Girl with A Snake

Surviving the Narcissist

by

Euraysia Duhaime

Table of Contents

Acknowledgements

This project wouldn't have been possible without the amazing support of my parents, they gave me life, and they saved my life. My therapist K, the reason I found myself and the reason I am still here with you all today. My friend Michelle, who said to me, "The world is waiting for you to do something amazing, so do something amazing!" and encouraged me to complete this book, and ZG, truly my heart; without his support, this would have never come to fruition.

Intro

Hello darling! If you've picked up my book, I can safely assume you are on a healing journey or looking to learn more about the insidious nature of narcissistic abuse. If neither applies, your reason is still valid, and I hope through my journey, you learn something, anything that can help you evolve into your higher self.

I can't tell you how many times I've rewritten this intro, first, in hopes of sounding like a writer. Then 2^{nd,} edit in hopes of sounding more like a survivor. 3rd edit, to sound less wounded, and here we are on the 4th edit, authentically me.

I've pushed down the initial intro but didn't erase it because "what if" says my anxiety. But I'm writing a new intro without glancing at the old one.

As I write this, I have my dog at my feet, Night at the Museum, playing in the background so I can focus better. I'm between work right now, so I can take some time alone to refocus and publish this egg I've been sitting on since 2018.

A journal and lessons. Lessons I've gone over and over in my head. New lessons were learned, and old lessons evolved and adopted new meanings. Transforming the lens through which I see these tower moments and accompanying lessons from a lens of trauma to one of the trauma responses, to one of hurt, then healing. It's been a very long, very difficult journey. At times I thought myself crazy, trying to reconcile two different beliefs in my mind, trying to rationalize the irrational. It's enough to make anyone crazy! But it wasn't me, it was a journey of going through and surviving abuse, Narcissistic abuse.

Narcissistic Abuse

Let me start by saying it is not your fault that you landed in this situation or ended up with a Narcissist or toxic person. It is not your fault.

I cannot stress this enough. We tend to internalize the abuse; what did we do, what could we do, what can we do better? We rationalize it; it's not his fault, s/he has trauma, s/he's been hurt, s/he has issues, it's mental illness, addiction, whatever the case may be.

Narcissistic abuse starts subtly, even before the relationship begins. There is usually a chaser and a runner. The chaser may have issues with abandonment and self-worth, and the runner is the Narcissist. Oftentimes, the pattern is that the Narcissist will string you along, playing the in-and-out game. Connecting for short bursts to make you feel good and feel special, but then confuse you by not wanting commitment. They will test your boundaries and see how much they can get away with without actually committing. Every time they ghost you, you internalize. Then every time they come back in is when they feel you detaching. Then one day, the magic happens! They choose you. The day has come, and those feelings of inadequacy are finally squashed, and you feel loved and validated.

Why did you put up with this? Maybe because you have a distorted view of what love is or should be. You possibly have an anxious attachment style and complex post-traumatic stress disorder (c-PTSD). Your upbringing may have taught you that red flags are safe, and what is safe is dangerous.

So now you're honeymooning with the Narcissist. Once the Narcissist feels it's time, and it's usually early, they will find an anchor. Maybe you move in together, maybe you get a pet, maybe there is a pregnancy involved, or maybe some financial entanglements. But there is always an anchor, something the Narcissist can use against you should you choose to respect yourself and leave.

The first time the Narcissist hurts you, you work it out because of the anchor. Be it substances, cheating, emotional or physical abuse, the Narcissist uses personal trauma to plead a case, swears up and down s/he will change, and you make it work. The Narcissist convinces you that you are loved, important, and love bombs you. You feel that sense of validation again, that love you felt you lost somehow. Your anxiety is soothed, and the reward is the relationship working out and the Narcissist's love and affection.

Enter the trauma bond. A trauma bond is an emotional bond created by a cyclical pattern of abuse perpetuated by intermittent reinforcement through rewards and punishments. This cycle might not be unfamiliar if you were raised with this pattern as a child or for an extended period of your life. The cycle of abuse that causes the trauma bond is in 4 stages:

stage 1: tension building
stage 2: incident of violence
stage 3: reconciliation
stage 4: calm

(https://psychcentral.com)

I want to note that trauma bonding is a tactic used by Narcissists to manipulate you, but trauma bonds can happen in any kind of relationship that have two people who haven't healed from whatever trauma drives toxic behaviours. Be it in relationships with parents, partners, or friends. Trauma bonds are not exclusive to romantic relationships.

Over time, the abuse gets worse and more evident, but by then, you have normalized, rationalized, and internalized the behaviours and abuse. You change yourself to accommodate the Narcissist to avoid arguments or to keep them happy, often at the expense of your own. Whenever you try to voice a concern or try to communicate, the Narcissist gets mad at you. The argument is filled with deflection, redirecting, blame-shifting, victim shaming, and eventually, you give up just to keep the peace, but not after some possible reactive abuse and a lot of damage.

Narcissistic abuse turns you into a shell of who you were. By the time you realize what you're dealing with, it's difficult to get out since your entire circle and existence have been shaped, moulded, and manipulated by this person. Your connections are severed or damaged, your self-esteem broken and shattered, your sense of self-worth nonexistent, and your confidence is destroyed.

I think of narcissistic abuse as a seed. There is that first argument, that first incident, that first fight and reunion, the seed is planted. Over time, the seed branches out, and consumes you like a weed. Reaching every part of your body and soul, and by the time you realize how sick you are, you're so entangled you feel like you can't get out or get free.

The process of healing is painful. You must understand the Narcissist and yourself in order to understand how you got into that position. Understand the individual you are dealing with, the traits that first attracted you, and why you are searching for those traits in someone else. Assess your attachment style and why it developed. Assess, accept and understand and heal any mental health afflictions or toxic traits you may have, and any childhood traumas you haven't addressed. You have to heal, rewire your brain and build yourself back up from the bottom. You have to redirect the pathways that you have been following that led you to where you are and create new healthy ones. Change you coping mechanism, adopt coping skills and strategies and touch on the things you've been avoiding or even unaware of your entire life.

Make no mistake, narcissistic abuse causes brain damage. This is how damaging it is. Being subject to any long-term abuse will cause your brain to overdevelop certain parts and under develop others. There truly is a physiological aspect to abuse. Being in such a volatile and abusive relationship, you are consistently living in a flight, fight, freeze or fawn state. Your nervous system is always on high alert. This causes an increase in cortisol in your body which wreaks havoc on your nervous system. The Hippocampus, the part of the brain associated mainly with learning and memory, is especially sensitive to the damaging effects of emotional distress, stress, and cortisol. When affected by cortisol, the Hippocampus shrinks. The cortisol also affects the Amygdala, which regulates emotions. So as the Hippocampus is shrinking, the Amygdala is stimulated, which forces us into more emotional responses and less able to learn or act with our rational mind. This is why sometimes it's difficult to remember parts of a situation that happened; because the trauma was so severe that the brain blocks out the memory as a defense mechanism. In the name of self preservation and protection.

There are times in my relationship where I can picture parts of N's outbursts so clearly, but then parts of the incident are blank. I can't remember how it ended or started or parts in the middle. This is because the event was so traumatic that my mind blocked out the parts that were too much for my brain to process. Similar patchy memory of an event that caused a concussion.

It's crucial that during your healing phase, you find an outside source that can guide you. You will not be able to grow using the same unhealed mind that got you into such an abusive relationship in the first place. Not only do you need guidance, but you need support. The process of healing and growth can be very difficult. It is painful, it is lonely, it is frustrating, and it can drive people mad. You have to dig deep and assess all those childhood wounds that feed insecurities and inadequacies that lead to anxiety and seeking behaviours, that then land you in toxic relationships. This process is difficult and earth-shattering, and support is integral in being able to process and heal. I can't tell you how healing it is to know, as awful as it is, that someone else has gone through the same things I have. That I'm not crazy and feel heard, validated, and a little less alone, ashamed, and isolated. Never underestimate the power of community and togetherness. Support groups work for a reason, but you have to be willing to take that first step to decide to heal and embrace vulnerability.

It is also worth noting that not everyone is ready to heal. I believe that we ascend every 2 years or so, into a higher version of ourselves (or we are meant to). However, if we are unable to self-reflect, see our role in situations, learn from them, and grow, our Karmic lessons will be put in our path over and over again in different vessels. Some people have trauma responses that inhibit

9

their ability to clearly self-reflect and see their role in situations. Rather, their version of self-reflection may be stewing on the subject until they are at a boiling point, full of resentment and then come back to defend, deflect and shift blame. Some people have so much trauma that they simply aren't able to see the lessons and therefore end up replaying the same cycle in different forms until that one breaking point. Some people are scared to heal because they aren't ready to open that pandora's box of personal pain. All any this does is prolong your suffering and keeps away the true blessings and abundance that is meant for you. This is because you've shown Source somehow, that you aren't ready to accept and appreciate, or maintain the abundance extended to you. Healing isn't comfortable. At the beginning of my healing journey, I'd leave therapy with puffy eyes and a need to lie down and take a nap to settle my nervous system. But the gifts it brings, the amazing change in myself, my surroundings, my voice, my confidence, and my entire life has come as a result of digging deep and doing that hard work. I encourage everyone to get therapy (if able). Even if you think there is nothing wrong with you! Because I guarantee you'll grow from it with the right therapist and the right therapy.

Narcissistic Personality disorder vs. a Toxic person.

Per the DSM, NPD includes:

A pervasive pattern of grandiosity (fantasy or behavior), need for admiration, and lack of empathy, beginning by early adulthood, as indicated by at least five of the following:

- Has a grandiose sense of self-importance (e.g., exaggerates achievements, expects to be recognized as superior without actually completing the achievements).
- Is preoccupied with fantasies of success, power, brilliance, beauty, or perfect love.
- Believes that they are "special" and can only be understood by or should only associate with other special people (or institutions).
- Requires excessive admiration.

- Has a sense of entitlement, such as an unreasonable expectation of favorable treatment or compliance with his or her expectations.
- Is exploitative and takes advantage of others to achieve their own ends.
- Lacks empathy and is unwilling to identify with the needs of others.
- Is often envious of others or believes that others are envious of them.
- Shows arrogant, haughty behaviors and attitudes.

The list forgot charming, pathological liars and able to adapt to any situation, given there is some sort of vested interest.

There has also been some debate about whether a Narcissist is able to feel empathy. Personally, I believe so. See, empathy is a spectrum. On one end, you have the Narcissist with a considerably basic ability to empathize. They can recognize you are feeling a certain way, and that you are having an emotional reaction (cognitive empathy). For instance, someone is crying during a movie, a Narcissist is likely to not understand why, "it's just a movie, it's not real." Here we see there are two important components missing, emotional empathy and compassionate empathy. Emotional empathy is the emotion that is invoked that drives compassionate empathy, which is the action that is taken as a result. An empath, on the other hand, can feel the full spectrum of the empathy scale. An Empath is able to relate, connect and understand not only the situation but every different reaction to the situation that an individual may feel in such an instance and may even take on some of that energy. Regardless of the situation, the Empath can feel and relate to the other person, whereas the Narcissist, being very basic in their range, cannot. The Narcissist therefore cannot connect all the necessary pieces together to understand the situation entirely and has little to no effect on them. This being said, there are many different kinds of individuals who display narcissistic traits and can be co morbid with personality disorders. Such as a Sociopathic Narcissist or a Psychopathic Narcissist. But not all people who have NPD are like these two aforementioned types.

Relationships with a Narcissist are very one-sided as well. It is about catering to the Narcissist and their needs to maintain a less turbulent and volatile home. As I mentioned, you, as the Narcissist's supply and victim, are consistently living in that fight, flight, freeze or fawn state, so keeping the chaos to a minimum is your goal. A happy home is totally off your radar. You just want to keep it down and managed to a rumbling boil. Relationships are also transactional with the Narcissist. It isn't about how much they care because of who you are as an individual, but rather how much they care is directly related to how much you have to offer them and how easily you are controlled by them. Additionally, nothing you have to offer will ever be enough. Even if you manage to check all the boxes, the bar will constantly be raised or moved and out of reach and always unreasonable and random.

The relationship will leave you depleted, lost, a shell of yourself. You'll be shocked at how your physical/mental/emotional health and appearance deteriorate as the Narcissist syphons your energy. Weight loss, or gain, depending on your reactions to stress. Your shine dulls, your voice silenced, your connections lost, severed, or damaged, and the next thing you know, you don't recognize yourself. By then, you may have tried to leave multiple times, planning, imagining, and setting goals, but with every almost attempt, you can picture the backlash, and you abandon the plan. Some people may be fortunate enough to be able to leave, but others need that one critical moment in the relationship, that one massive tower moment, that moment where the universe, Source, push it to the limit because you aren't learning and you're sent that critical incident and moment that forces your hand some way or somehow.

For me, it was the arrest. That was the moment I knew I was out. But with a Narcissist, it's never over. The poking, instigating, and manipulation. I'm one of the lucky ones. Regardless of how bad the exit was, he couldn't (in theory) contact me. He had a no-contact order. With the exception of a few incidents, the threat of possible jail time kept him (mostly) at bay. The locks were changed, the victim's program provided me with an emergency phone, HR at work gave me accommodations and we created a safety plan, my neighbours kept an eye out for me, and I had a motion detection camera facing the entrance to my building and parking lot. Even with all these measures in place, there were a few breaches. Every time, all the police could do was give him warnings. The system is undoubtedly broken, but that is the system in which I was required to navigate. This is why you need to be proactive and hold hard boundaries with a Narcissist, but this is so difficult to do when you are still working through the trauma.

Do Narcissists seek help? Can they be helped?

Sometimes, but not often. This is the reason NPD goes underdiagnosed. Narcissists don't typically get help or seek therapy because they do not believe there is anything wrong with them. Seeking therapy would be admitting they're flawed, and that is not on a Narcissist's radar. To them, everyone else is the problem, and others just have to accommodate them!
I remember after an argument one night, in order to end the argument, I finally pleaded with N to tell me what he wanted in order to end the argument. He said, "I want you to repeat after me. 'N, you are perfect the way you are, and there is nothing you need to change'". I repeated that back to him verbatim, and he said, "See, now, was that so hard?" and the argument was over. When you think of what it takes to appease a Narcissist, this is a prime example.
A Narcissist believes that they are perfect, the most intelligent, the most evolved version of themselves, and the one others should emulate. They are above the law, and rules don't apply to them. Especially not their own. This profound lack of ability to self reflect prevents the Narcissist from realizing they are the problem, the reason and the cause for pain and abuse. Becoming better for someone else is not typically on their list of reason to seek help.

If a Narcissist does seek therapy, there are a few (this is by no means an exhaustive list) reasons why and it is usually for self serving reasons. A Narcissist may go to therapy to learn more about NPD to be able to use terms and tactics to their advantage. The Narcissist may seek therapy as a means to improve their image and solidify the narrative that they are the victim. The Narcissist may seek therapy because they have hit their version of "rock bottom" and are afraid of losing what they have or their comforts. Keep in mind, most Narcissists don't have a version of rock bottom because there is always someone there to bail them out, but if they do hit rock bottom, which includes financial and material loss, they may be spurred into therapy in order to gain back and maintain that which they have lost. Helping other people is typically an inconvenience to a Narcissist, especially if there is nothing in it for them and there is typically some element of control or retaining control involved in their reason for seeking help.

Another important point I should make is never to try a couple's counselling with a Narcissist. They will likely quit early and blame the therapist (s/he was unqualified, I could do a better job, they didn't know what they were talking about, all s/he did was take your side, etc.) It will rarely end well, and they will seldomly change.

Toxic people

We've all met one and likely have been one. With information on narcissistic abuse and Narcissistic Personality Disorder out there, it seems like everyone is ready to label all toxic people as Narcissists. But as we see above, Narcissism is a disorder. Not everyone who is toxic is a Narcissist and this is a very important point to remember.

To differentiate, we must dig deeper, look at the drive, the seed that causes toxic people to display toxic behaviours. Most toxic people have some sort of trauma or distorted upbringing that has caused them to develop coping mechanisms and trauma responses. Not having the right guide, therapy, outlets, or information, these responses become part of them.

Take myself, for example! All my life, I was told I was expressive, over the top, a great storyteller, and I should be in acting, etc. Why? Because I was expressive and comical. I could retell a story, re-enact all the emotions, the highs and the lows, and make people feel what I was feeling, which is what the people in the story were feeling. But put me in front of a crowd or on a stage, and I was the worst! I was criticized by my drama teacher in high school

14

regularly and had trouble during auditions when I tried acting later in life. I was too shy and/or insecure. I wasn't able to break out of my shell enough to be a convincing actor! So why was I so good at storytelling? It was a trauma response.

I spent a lifetime supressing my emotions. A by-product of generational trauma. So naturally, when it was my turn to express myself through what other people felt or re-enacting another situation, I was able to express emotions freely and I did so with such sincerity! I was able to express emotions without fear of reprimand or shame. Imagine finally being able to express the frustration or sadness or anger you've felt through a situation and you know won't get you in "trouble". That became a part of my character, my personality. But it wasn't my character or personality. It was a toxic trait. A trauma response

The same came to validation. I always sought outside validation. That came out in attention-seeking behaviours, a need to be seen. I chased things that I hated, like modeling and sought the attention of men or people I had no interest in. And once I got it, I was bored, and the mission was over. Was this because I was a Narcissist? No, but I was displaying toxic traits. I had an anxious attachment style and I acted out of unhealed trauma.

I viewed love and affection as something that was earned, not given. I was guided by trying to show that I was worthy of love, and usually, that was gained by what I looked like or what I could offer rather than who I was as a person. How could I possibly be loved for who I was on the inside when I wasn't even sure of who I was (I thought). Almost all the parts of my character were driven or moulded by some kind of trauma. I was basically a walking red flag, and I had no idea! Deep down, I'd still do anything and everything for my friends (people pleasing) and ask for nothing in return (guilty soul). It hurt when they didn't reciprocate the friendship, but that didn't stop me from bending over backwards. If anything, that caused me to do even more. I was terrified of showing people who I truly was in case they would think I was weird due to my afflictions, so I was the person they expected me to be and mirrored without even realizing it. Naturally, this caused me even more anxiety over my already crippling anxiety, and I masked even harder so people wouldn't notice I was struggling. The topic of mental health was (and is) so stigmatized, and I struggled in silence during my formative high school years when the need for acceptance and validation was high and where I was still trying to find and form my own personal identity.

I thought of myself as adaptable and able to get along with any group. A social butterfly who could blend in with any crown and be friends with all types of people. But that was because I was always moulding and masking to suit my environment. I never had a solid opinion on issues because my views changed with every group I was with for fear of thinking "would I sound stupid?" or "Would they see me as disagreeable?" (insecurity & need for validation), "Would they stop liking me?" (insecurity and abandonment issues). No wonder Karma followed me around; I had no idea who I was. No sense of who my authentic self was, or what I truly valued. My fluid identity was a result of not having one at all. No stable, grounded sense of self that guided my decisions, thoughts, responses, and opinion. No solid moral or ethical groundwork to guide me. That mess led me to attract very narcissistic and toxic people whom I followed blindly, and I did anything to maintain their friendship, even to my own detriment or to the detriment of others.

Looking back now, I see the pattern of Narcissists and toxic people in my life, and I know exactly why they were put there and the lessons I did/did not learn. I followed these friends and swore my loyalty to them even though loyalty was not a concept they valued. When I didn't learn the very hurtful and necessary lessons, the good and gracious Source planted N in my life. Source knew all I wanted was love, a family, and that was the only medium that would force me into the deep pain it takes to finally break, heal, and grow.

Here is where the toxic person wakes up. Realizes, "Oh dang… that's me. My bad! I need to do better! I see my role in the situation. Am I the Narcissist? Am I the problem?" And right there, we can determine, most often, that the Toxic person is not a Narcissist. Why? A Narcissist will not often wonder if they are a Narcissist or the root of the problem at hand. The Narcissist will rarely decide to grow and be better, especially not for the sake of other people because s/he does not find any benefit in helping others or improving the welfare of others unless it directly benefits them. To be better for other people, to genuinely heal, is not often a top priority and besides, what is there to heal? They're amazing as they are.

Toxic people or people with unhealed trauma will display narcissistic or toxic traits. It can be very easy to forget that others have things going on in the background as well. To remember that other people also have issues and concerns, and stressors that they hide but affect their every thought and action.

The cashier that you thought was rude may be wondering how she's getting home from work that day because her gas tank is empty.

That person who blew past you in a rush without apologizing may be having a panic attack and needed to get out and get air.

That friend who was short with you today may be battling substance abuse and has a shorter fuse today than others because they are balancing stressors and possible relapse.

That person who seems like they are leading with ego may just be acting on a trauma response to over-explain because they felt unheard as a child.

That friend that consistently cuts you off and makes it seem like the conversation is all about them, may be struggling with ADHD, and this is their way of showing you that they are listening and can relate.

There are so many factors to consider when interacting with individuals, and it is crucial that we lead with an empathic heart rather than ignorance and ego. Just because a person does something toxic or displays a red flag doesn't make them a Narcissist and doesn't mean they are unable to grow. Instead of judging, let's try a little more understanding. Kindness, understanding, love and patience can change lives.

Leaving the Narcissist

Sometimes the exit is just as dangerous, if not more dangerous, than the relationship itself. One of the main reasons people stay is because they cannot leave and are trapped. Maybe because after the breakup, a final breakup, the Narcissist is mad, embarrassed, forced to create a new narrative, put out, inconvenienced, and feels or is afraid of being outed. You know who s/he really is, and you don't fall for their games or their lies anymore and they've lost control of you and the situation. When someone is manipulative, vengeful, angry, and determined to save their image, the fallout can be awful, dangerous, and messy. My heart goes out to you if you have children with a Narcissist. This is why recovery is important, crucial, and lifesaving!

Everyone has a struggle when trying to make an exit, but the one thing we all have in common is the fear of the judgement and the opinions of others. I remember being told by a friend once, not to talk to them anymore until N was out of my life. That would be excellent if I was able to get him out of my life! The literal goal! But I couldn't just kick him out due to financial, but also safety reasons. If I left, I'd have no place to stay, no shelter, no solution and no safety or protection from him. If my friends couldn't take me in, then who was offering to go to co-sign for an apartment or provide my first and last? Who would help me move and help me pay the moving costs?

It's easy to tell someone what to do when you have zero invested and no responsibility or obligation attached. I know, I was once that person. The person that said, "everyone has an option, and a person can always leave whenever they feel like it." Well, Source knew I wouldn't learn my lesson unless I totally understood the gravity of the situation. Pure Karma that I landed into that very situation, but also a much-needed lesson for me to grow and discover myself and heal.

Remember that unless they are a part of the solution, the opinions of the people that judge you are of zero value. It's easy when on the outside to look in and point out all the options you believe someone has, but keep in mind, no matter how much they tell you, they withhold information they may be scared to share, and therein lies the real danger they face.

I was very lucky to be afforded assistance, support and trauma therapy so I could move through the phases of grief and healing with guidance. I was also very fortunate that N was forced from my home, and the removal was not optional for him. Then I had to find out who I was at the core of my being. Not just heal but discover and evolve. There was a lot of growing and ascending which was done in a very short time frame which is exhausting and mentally draining, but life changing! In that process, on that journey, I realized that woman, the one who dated the Narcissist, was a fundamentally broken and confused version of myself. I didn't want to be her or the woman she was before she met him. Healing wasn't about going back to who I was; that was the individual that got me into those toxic relationships in the first place. I entered therapy wanting to heal my inner child and enjoy the journey to finding who I was and wanted to become. Not to put the broken pieces back together, but use some of those broken pieces, the ones that held valuable lessons and traits like kindness, empathy and generosity, and collage them together with new, more stable, and healed pieces. To keep the base and foundation of who I was, but grow, evolve, and develop into a better version of myself that would make better decisions, learn to be confident and love herself.

The Why?

Why am I sharing my journal? My actual diary? Because I felt alone, and I don't want anyone to feel that way. I want to share what I've learned and hope that it helps someone else. Helps someone else get through a tough situation, deal with internalization, or just learn how to end the cycle. All the above and everything in between. I feel very blessed that I received the help and therapy that I did and I wish more people had access to learn what I learned and help themselves. Help themselves get out safely, find the confidence to use their voice, find themselves and love themselves, and heal so to help others heal.

That is my why. That is my wish.

That through this journey with me, from my past to my present, you use these lessons on your healing journey, expand on them, and turn that love and healing energy outwards and help others do the same. Encourage others find their self-confidence, their authentic self, and their self-love and share that with the world. To be the catalyst for others.

This world needs more empathetic hearts. More people to lead with love and show the world that vulnerability is a strength, not a weakness and being your most authentic, healing self is the way to happiness.

The Who?

Who am I? Well, this section has changed over and over since the beginning of this journey. Isn't it always difficult to describe who you are? Sometimes you feel ashamed, sometimes too vulnerable, "am I sharing too much?", "what do I say?", "what do I like?". As it turns out, we feel anxious and self-conscious because we don't know ourselves or aren't confident in ourselves! We are not living in our authentic selves, and therefore we mask. We mirror. Consistently and subconsciously asking ourselves, "what do I think these ppl expect/want me to say/hear?" and then we adopt that persona. We almost treat it like a test question and try to figure out what the right answer is.

So, who am I?

So far, I've learned that I'm simple, introverted, and always healing. I'm open to new experiences, though my crippling anxiety sometimes tells me otherwise. I love trying new food, but only when

I can share it with someone else. I love animals, always have, and always will. I'm a sucker for a Mastiff or Bully breed, though my favourite babies are a lab/shep mix and a husky.

I am spiritual and religious. I go to Church, but not all the time. I have a great relationship with my Priest and enjoy our short talks after Mass, where I pick his brain. I'm strong on my virtues, values, and ethics, and this is what drives me and my actions and goals. I am developing my spiritual and intuitive abilities and believe that there is so much more out there than we can understand, and energy connects us all.

I've always been good at sports or at least I felt like I was. I was very competitive, and never did well in school; that is until I learned why. I simply didn't learn how they expected me to or taught me to. Now, I can see that it was also part anxiety and trauma, not specifically in that order or in equal parts. However, once I received therapy, I did very well in University and started to love school. Reading and learning are now at the center of my soul, and sharing what I learn is at the center of my heart.

I hope this journey through my life, my mind, my pain, and my lessons brings you some peace, healing, understanding of self, and self love.

The What?

I'm sure you're wondering by this part, when am I going to give you the "what"? What happened? What was my experience? Well, in short, I met a guy who seemed like he wanted a relationship and then said he didn't. He strung me along for a little while until he decided he was ready. We started dating, and things moved quickly. In no time, we had a puppy, and I had given up my apartment. And then things started to go poorly. The puppy was the anchor. He knew very well my affinity for animals and wanting something to mother and love. Shortly after we got the puppy, he cheated. That moment began the cycle and created the trauma bond. He convinced me he was sorry, and we worked it out. The same thing would happen over and over, and I would always believe him when he said he wanted to do better, give up the substances, start fresh. And he would, for a couple of weeks. Then they cycle started again. Convinced that it was the city, we moved; changed towns. Left the city and moved to where I was from, not far but distanced enough from the city to give me false sense of hope. It was a fresh start. To him, there we were with a new circle for him to reinvent himself in and syphon from. The same cycles continued in the new town with the new people and a new environment. It was a fresh start and a fresh place to begin all over again for him. New friends to fool and new people to manipulate. I admit I played a huge role in the situation. I enabled the behaviours. I didn't have the confidence to stand up for myself. I had traumas and an inner child I hadn't healed.

But there were other factors. More insidious factors.

Why didn't I leave?

That's the most harmful question you can ask someone in a an abusive relationship. It doesn't take into consideration the complexity of abuse and how deeply ingrained it is.

There was a long list of things that prevented me from being able to leave. For starters, we had a dog together and that pup was my crutch, my emotional support, and my baby of babies. I raised him, cared for him from 6 weeks of age. To separate me from my baby would break me, and he knew that and used that threat every chance he could.

He also owed me a lot of money, which he would give to me in increments and take it off what he owed, and he would only release the funds if he approved what I was using the money for. Holding me financially hostage. If I needed money to go to a birthday party, he would give me some money, write a new contract, adjust the balance, and have me sign 2 copies. One for him and one for me.

How did he owe me so much money? It started when I went back to school. N had convinced me to stop working while I was in school. He said he saw how much I was splitting my time, and if I agreed to quit and stay home, be with him, take care of the dogs and focus on my studies, he would take care of the rent and help me wherever I need. I had been working steady since I was 12 years old right through college and my first degree, so being able to focus solely on my studies and take care of the dogs was amazing! His imitation sincerity was so convincing, and he knew just what to say to play to my heartstrings.

To save money while I was in school, we moved into a school-owned building with lower rent and more flexible payments. He went almost 10 months without paying rent which was charged to my student account. I ended up racking up almost $10 000 on my student account which prevented me from graduating. I didn't learn from that either. I kept putting bills under my name which he never paid, and I ended up with crippled credit. He made 3x what I made monthly and could have paid me off quickly if he wanted to. Funds and his ability to pay me were never the issue, it was all about control.

He also played a huge role in damaging and severing ties as well. He isolated me and managed to convince me that my friends and family were awful and he was my only true source of support. After years of manipulation, trauma bonding, and disintegration of my self-esteem, I began to believe him, and the relationships with my friends and family deteriorated.

He had essentially created a world where I was truly crippled and dependent oh him in all ways. I wasn't able to move even if I wanted to. I had no help, no support, and no access to funds. Even if I had funds, I couldn't find an apartment with my credit or one that would take my dogs. And how would I approach the issue of leaving without him losing his mind? His tantrums were scary. He was scary. And volatile, vengeful, unpredictable, and addicted to substances. To up and leave suddenly was too unsafe and not possible without finances and a co signer. I had neither.

Aside from the obvious and overt shows of violence, N had a way of instilling fear in subtle ways. For instance, N kept calling me his wife when convenient after the breakup. Correcting him led to issues and awkwardness and a need to explain which I didn't want to get into. If I corrected him in front of people, that showed he was lying which was damaging to his image and unacceptable and had consequences. So, I didn't. He would use these tactics when we were out with or ran into other people. Like when we were out with his boss and his wife and their friends. He would invite me to these events to look like a wholesome, honest guy. Saying no wasn't an option either. If I didn't go, he'd come home flying and I'd have to deal with whatever the fallout was. If I went, at least I could try to end the night before things got out of hand and at a reasonable hour. Going with him was more for my safety and security than anything. He also played the role when we were in a situation where he felt challenged. Like when we were out and there was another man present like a male Teller at the bank. I kept playing the housewife role too because I didn't want any issues at home. I didn't need the stress. I needed to make it one day at a time until he moved out. Keep things civil to avoid any vindictive, resentful backlash.

Finally, we broke up. I don't even remember how, but we did. After the breakup, N decided he was going to move out and I would keep our dog since I was his main caregiver and N simply didn't have the time. He kept telling me that he would move out, and he never did. He kept pushing the date back, saying he had a plan. He has all sorts of plans like buying a trailer or a tiny home. It was one excuse after another, one idea after another. Asking led to issues, temper tantrums and threats. So, I stopped asking and just waited. He never moved out. He lived with me for almost a year until he was removed.

It came to a crumbling end when N was arrested. One night, in his true fashion, he was mad that I was upset. I was upset because he stood me up for an appointment to view a car. He said if he approved of the car, he would pay the down payment using some the money he owed me and then adjust the balance. Naturally, he didn't show up, came home inebriated, and things escalated. As N got home, I was folding laundry and visibly upset. I had expressed how upset I was over text earlier that night but that didn't bother him. What bothered him was that I was still upset when he came home. I wasn't sure what he thought would happen, but he definitely thought I'd be over it. He cornered me on the couch, trying to intimidate me into believing he was sober. The exchange was getting dangerous, so I left to go down to the laundry room, where he followed me and became physical. He threatened to harm on me, our dog, followed me around the apartment, and then he finally allowed me to retire to my room, but not before getting physical with our dog too. He slammed the bedroom door shut and wouldn't let me out for almost 5 hours. Yelling, screaming, banging the door, and threatening me the entire time. The almost 5 hours I was stuck in my room until the police arrived was spent on the phone with a police dispatcher and a couple of friends. Whoever would answer my call at that hour. I had to be on the phone with someone. Knowing I was talking to someone kept him from getting too out of hand. It meant he knew someone else could hear him. It was my safety, my protection piece, my insurance. He had no idea I was on the phone with the police as I pretended it was my friend and start talking as such when he would barge in before leaving and slamming the door again.

Eventually, he was arrested and charged with Forcible Confinement defined in the Criminal Code of Canada as depriving an individual of the liberty to move from one point to another by unlawfully confining, imprisoning, or forcibly seizing that person. A conviction would mean imprisonment of up to 10 years. He was released on a promise to appear, and I hid at a friend's house with my dogs for almost two weeks until I felt ready to return to my apartment.

After N was arrested, he came back and took our dog. There were firm legal conditions that outlined how to collect his belongings and what that consisted of. We had to agree to a time and date first and foremost. As he was not allowed to contact me (he had a peace bond to follow), it had to be coordinated with the police and/or the investigating detective. I would then leave the apartment during the date and time agreed upon. He would then be escorted by police with my father present, and he could only collect items that were indisputable in ownership like anything with his name on it, ie: mail. Instead, it was communicated that he made a false claim to the police department, and they escorted him over when I wasn't home. I came home to him trying to break into my apartment by pushing my A/C through my window with 2 other people and 2 police officers watching. I was told that he claimed we had gotten into an argument, and I locked him out. I was also told that he had claimed to have installed he A/C himself and that was why they were allowing him to push it in and enter through that window. None of it made any sense. Little did N know, when my father had installed the A/C for me, he bolted it to the windrow frame in case an incident like this which is why he couldn't get in that way.

In the confusion, sheer panic, and under instruction of the officers, I opened my apartment door, N pushed his way into the apartment, my dog ran out, and he took him and disappeared down the street. When he came back, the officers forced me to allow him to take our dog. The more I tried to explain the situation, the more backlash I got from the officers. It was his word against mine, and they sided with him. As N was acting with their consent, I couldn't claim any wrongdoing by him specifically; only the officers (which I did). He was spiteful, embarrassed, and angry that he had lost control. Now people would know what he did. He felt outed and was hell bent on hurting me in the deepest way possible. The only way to do that was to use my dog.

No one wanted to go to trial and to avoid it, he was offered a peace bond and shared custody of our dog, which he refused. Our dog was the only element of control he had left. He had the easy way out and refused it! Due to his refusal, we were forced to go to trial where I would have to testify against him. The lead-up to the trial was awful. Friends left me, some promised to help, then bailed, some promised to help, then got angry, and the prep. The prep was awful. From re-reading the transcript of the police interview, reliving all the events from the incident(s), to the battle with the police department. It was trauma on top of trauma.

How did I get through it?

I had an amazing therapist! Kathy was a blessing. Due to the circumstances, I was offered trauma therapy via a victim's support program. I immediately clicked with Kathy. Her approach was very spiritually based, and she and I got along instantly. I still see her today, now in 2023. She has been the staple and root of my healing journey and my guidance through times that should have broken me. She was my sounding board when I needed to talk myself into an answer and mirrored myself back to me when I needed to do more self reflection and soul searching.

I took time and I really put in the work. I was indeed broken to the core and needed to rebuild. No one I knew back then was talking about narcissistic abuse. I had never heard of it, and I had no idea what I was dealing with. I threw myself down the rabbit hole. Read and watched everything I could on Narcissists, Narcissistic Abuse, Narcissistic Personality Disorder, Sociopaths, and Psychopaths. Emotional and mental abuse, financial abuse, childhood trauma, etc. I was determined to know better so I could be better and do better.

I realized the red flags I should have run from, but instead ran to. I pinpointed my attachment style and what it stemmed from. I broke down generational traumas, my childhood traumas, my unhealed inner child. I analyzed patterns and cycles I had. I also focused on my spirituality. I started doing Reiki sessions with an incredible medium and meditative yoga sessions with a stellar instructor. I was focused on my health, finding myself, and healing. I even moved, changed cities, and tried starting fresh.

On journeys like this, where you dive headfirst into your healing, the universe truly does reward you. I was making such great progress in my healing and the universe blessed me. I reconnected with a man I had always been in love with. We started dating and very quickly, moved in together. I focussed on him, helping him and made him the priority instead of prioritizing myself and my healing. Anything he needed; I was there to help. From home to work. Work did so good and grew so fast that we managed to buy a house! This relationship was everything my heart dreamt of, and I was supposed to enter it as the person I had worked so hard to become. Instead, I fell into those same old patterns and repeated the same unhealthy cycles. I reverted to the old, unhealed version of myself. I wasn't seeing Kathy regularly as the pandemic threw a wrench in our ability to coordinate sessions. I had no time to help myself and I stopped focussing on my recovery and gave everything to others. I worked jobs I needed rather than following my passions. I was living to make it through the day to help someone else and structured my day around someone else's routine. I hadn't learned from my Karmic relationship with N. Neither of us were perfect, we both had things we needed to work on, and communicating was difficult. I would react to him, and he would react to me. The fire just kept burning, and eventually we separated. I sold my part of the house and moved out into a small apartment with my lab to start all over again.

I realized I still had a lot of growing to do. I had to learn how to love and commit to myself as much as I do others and I dug deep to figure out the lessons that I needed to learn and relearn. The universe rewarded me for all the hard work I was doing, but I wasn't dedicated or healed enough to hold boundaries and put myself and my growth as a priority to maintain this abundance. So, it took it away. I had to spend time relearning old lessons, finding my confidence again, and dedicating myself to myself. Lead with the heart, not the head; follow my intuition and my guides and heal so I could bring my love and my gifts to the world. I also had to learn how to forgive and what forgiveness meant. This tumultuous journey provided me with important lessons so I could share them and help heal. My purpose is to heal, to help heal. To keep learning and evolving so I can help others through situations where they feel alone; but truly aren't. Just the same as I felt at one point in my journey.

[..] and italics are added to provide context or withhold/change identifying information, but were not part of the original journal entry. Names have been changed to protect Identity and privacy.

Chapter 1

Journal Entry

August 26, 2019

Decided to try this journal thing again. I was standing in the bathroom looking at my hair, playing with it and pulling on it and watching it just fall out and realized it's when I'm "deep thinking" that I play with my hair. I started to think that maybe that is my (albeit unhealthy) way that I process my stress and trauma, and I am trying to replace that habit with something new, like writing. I figure every time I feel like playing with my hair, I'll just turn to my journal. Dig deep and find out what it is at that moment that is causing me even the slightest stress or anxiety. I'll keep time stamps to assess when I'm writing and how much and this will also gauge my anxiety.

Yesterday, or last night rather, I kept thinking of when I would be able to get *my dog* back. "What the reunion would be like. What will happen September 5th with the court case? Will I be able to *get my dog* back then? How long will the criminal trial take? How much longer do I have to deal with this? Should I wait for the *3rd party police* investigation to be complete before I can try to get *my dog* back? How long does it take to investigate police and their wrongdoing?"

These questions just lead to more stress. More playing with my hair. Psoriasis flare-ups and picking and pulling; I hate those actions. I hate that I have associated negative coping mechanisms to those words and this makes me actually hate those words. There is now so much negativity associated with those words, those descriptors. Hopefully, I now have appropriate ways to process my trauma. Hopefully, I am now creating and reinforcing more appropriate ways to process my trauma.

Kathy is definitely helping me with that. I hope one day we can talk about therapy and counseling without associating it with any shame or weakness. I think everyone, at some point, should consider counselling. No one is perfect and we all have things we need to work on and improve, learn how to process in a more positive and appropriate way which I feel is getting more and more difficult considering the generation we live in. From parents who see therapy as a weakness to a generation that seeks "therapy" in the form of motivational quotes on social media that are very, and almost thoughtlessly reposted and then never revisited. We have created an emotionally unhealthy and unaware society. Social media has helped nurture Narcissists and people who live behind a highly curated version of themselves to prove to, and impress people they don't actually care for. Sad reality we live in now.

We need to teach that failure is ok and required to grow and that image does not equal value or good character, nor does it define you. To be true to who you are and to appreciate and learn how to process the entire range of human emotion so that people can live an emotionally healthy life and cope with loss, conflict, anger, frustration, trauma, hopelessness, and the like in an appropriate way. That is the person I am becoming. Someone aware of her feelings and emotions, with the ability to process them in a healthy way. I am becoming the best version of myself after 4 years of trauma and I am proud of that.

Lessons:

- BE VULNERABLE: I can't express how important it is to be your authentic self. The stress and anxiety that comes with always trying to mask or mirror or hide any single aspect of yourself is unhealthy and a root cause of disease. We often learn to mask because growing up, we were in a situation where we had to conform or mask to fit in. We never develop our own identities or felt free to do so. That kind of deeply ingrained trauma can cause ulcers, anxiety and can even escalate to an increased risk of cancer and other major physical illnesses or chronic diseases. These can all be related back to the constant stress of not finding and being your authentic and genuine self.

When I read this post, I thought about how much anxiety it used to give me if people found out about my hair. It was the worst! I even wore a wig when I had to testify at N's trial because I was ashamed. I was ashamed that I had lost my hair as a result of the stress and trauma that he caused me. Secondly, I didn't want him to have the satisfaction of seeing how much stress he had put me through, but shame trumped the latter.

As a woman, losing your hair is a different kind of traumatic. There are so many socially constructed standards of beauty that we try to live up to. We even have standards for what "messy" look like. How to make the perfect "messy bun" or how to style your PJs when you head to Walmart. The media has a never-ending stream of advice for women on how women should look. So naturally, when I started losing my hair, the shame and anxiety only made the hair loss worse. I hid it for a very long time. Then before the trial, I went and cut off my hair. I got a Pixie cut! It was cute, but you could still see the spots. So, my mom bought me a wig. Real hair, lace front, the ~$400 kind. I wore it every day. It was difficult with my hair, so I figured since I'm wearing it all the time anyways, I might as well shave my head. And I did. I BIC'd it right down to the skin. It was easier to wear the wig this way.

That was great for a hot minute, but the wig was itchy, my head would get rashes, and the glue was all a mess. So, I just let it all out there. I made a YouTube post about my hair and why I shaved my head, and I was honest with myself, my afflictions, and my healing. What happened next was truly amazing.

Friends that I never imagined having any issues or anxiety came forward! They had alopecia, or Trichotillomania, and they had difficulty coping too. Just the act of sharing and trusting enough to confide in someone relieves so much pressure, so much shame. That veil of shame is a little less heavy when you know you're not alone. You're not "crazy" or "weird." Someone else understands. That relief is intense and the first step towards healing.

Never underestimate the strength of the spark that is ignited when someone finds community.

- WE NEED TO EMPLOY BETTER COPING STRATEGIES: How difficult this journey is, how little skills many of us have, and how blissfully ignorant we are about it. We all cope differently; that's certain. The key is to find out what your coping mechanisms are and whether they are healthy, or self-sabotaging.

I used to believe that I coped well, but that was quite the illusion. I managed, but I didn't cope. To cope with something is to manage and overcome difficult situations. To be conscious of strategies used to reduce unpleasant emotions. Did I cope with situations? No, I managed them until the next one, or the same one arose. And when the situation did arise enough times, I broke down and did anything I could to manage that; the breakdown, not the situation. There was no healthy coping involved, no rest and digest for my nervous system. No way to balance out my emotions and moods. I had no outlets either; if I wasn't doing what N was doing, I wasn't present or giving him the much-needed attention he required. As in full attention. If I participated in hobbies, I felt so guilty or nervous that it would be an excuse and an out for him to go out and do what he did, which would then begin the cycle, which would then turn out bad for me. I lost my sense of self and my ability to cope. Everything was sending me into reaction mode.

Once his presence was no longer an issue, I had to learn to cope. To cope in all situations. What were my reactions? My actual reactions? What emotions or fears drove those, and how do I learn to regulate my emotions and process a situation?

My whole life, I employed an avoidant-focused coping strategy. I would avoid and distance myself from the issue. If you avoid it or ignore it, it's a nonissue, right?! Out of sight, out of mind. What did that turn me into? A quiet people pleaser, afraid to speak her truth and believed that love is to be earned, not given, and to earn it, you must be on your best behaviour and prove you deserved it.

Throughout my entire relationship, I tried to avoid situations which then enabled the behaviour that was so harmful and traumatizing. I changed the way I viewed what was happening in the relationship to make it make sense, to justify his actions, to rationalize everything, which then caused me to internalize everything.

Narcissistic abuse is a weed. That seed first planted by the initial abuse; the first time the Narcissist manipulates, and you allow it, enable it, and leave it unaddressed. Or maybe even it was unnoticed by you because you have a distorted, conditioned view of love and relationships and didn't even consider the first instance as abusive. From that seed, every time you internalize, every time to avoid the situation, every time to tiptoe, enable, take the blame, allow your self-esteem to be crushed, or play small, that seed grows. In no time, the weed has branched out and consumed every part of your being. It affects your physical health, your mental health, and your emotional health. By the time you realize the damage, this weed has strangled your sense of self. Created a new foundation of pathways for the Narcissist's poison to travel through your entire being.

Identifying this, understanding this, and utilizing healthy coping strategies is crucial in being able to change the situation. You can then begin the change from this fear-based, avoidant coping strategy to a more constructive one. A strategy that is rooted in reducing stress, identifying triggers and where they stem from and responding vs reacting. But how do we get there?

- FIND YOUR VOICE: Not an easy task. We all think we've found our voice when we're young, then our new voice in our 20s. Then we think we know who we truly are in our 30s. But I'll tell you a little secret, at 38 years old, I'm finally finding mine!

Did I seem like I had a voice before? Yes! But I was the Queen of masking. I was also a great storyteller and could capture an audience. My parents used to always tease that I should have gone into acting. And I did. I tried, and it wasn't for me. I couldn't act! What I could do, was feel the feelings I felt when incidents happened or feel the emotions other people felt during certain situations, and I would then be free to re-tell and display those emotions without reprimand or judgement. It was a strange but useful way to express my feelings or feel feelings without fear that someone would feel attacked, or get defensive, or fear that I would get "in trouble" for expressing how I felt. I also felt like people were more inclined to listen when I told it as a story, rather than explaining my own hurt, pain and frustration. I wasn't like this all the time or with everyone. Turns out this is a trauma response as a result of suppressing my emotions most of my life. This made me hyper-emotional when I was able to show emotion in a place or circumstance where I felt safe. Whether I was being too emotional over a situation, or through story telling. If it was through story telling, it was a way of me being able to feel emotions after the fact, so people would be able to understand how I felt at the time, but also laugh at the event/reaction/situation in hindsight, rather than get upset or reactive in the moment (if they were involved).

When N and I ended, and I started to unearth all these things. I started to find my confidence and use my voice. It took courage. Courage in accepting who I was, the good and the flawed, and being comfortable with letting people see it. It took learning to express how I felt effectively and appropriately and being confident in my opinions and thoughts. Putting myself and my emotional and mental health first, and setting and holding boundaries with people, places, and things to protect that. This was hard. I consistently second-guessed my opinions and decisions. I had to remind myself that what I thought was normal was possibly toxic, and what I thought was toxic was likely normal. I had to get comfortable with being uncomfortable. For someone with high anxiety, this is enough to make you mad. But I did it! I found the courage to be authentically me through forcing myself to break my comfort zones regardless of how much anxiety it caused because I knew the end result would benefit me rather than hurt me.

- CONFIDENCE TAKES PRACTICE: The turning point was when I shaved my head. I had nothing left to hide. I was still anxious about it. I was always anxious about it. I always thought, "That person is staring… that person must be thinking xyz… those people are snickering…". But I practiced being confident every time I went out. I didn't try to hide under hats. I wore my baldness proudly (if even just faking it). If my hair started to come in, but was patchy, I was ok with it. I stopped trying to hide or cover it up, and I embraced it. I started walking with my head up rather than down, looking at people rather then at the ground. I had to rewire my thinking which took so much out of me that I was consistently exhausted, but I knew deep down that was only temporary.

No hair? Great – easier to put the cream on.

No hair? No worries! Now people can see the earrings I wear!

No hair? Great, let's buy bold lipstick and draw attention there!

I used to hate that old saying, "fake it till you make it," but I now see the validity in it. Especially when it comes to building confidence, and once you are confident, you won't need or want the validation of others. You don't need the approval of others. You are confident in yourself, in your stance, in your morals and values and ethics, and you don't need any outside validation which means you won't seek it elsewhere with unhealthy behaviours. This is when you will be able to stand tall and be confident in your voice and your authentic self. This is when the magic happens! But this is also the loneliest part of your healing journey. People tend to shy away from people who are authentically themselves, who know, express, and stand behind their morals and values everyday. Whether its because others feel uncomfortable with anything different than their conditioned norms, whether it's because you being authentic and genuine may trigger parts of themselves they don't like, or if your light intimidates them, etc. Don't let the fear or people falling out keep you from being your authentic self and shining your true light, and using your voice to speak your truth.

One of the most difficult parts of this journey was using my voice once I found it. I would sometimes offend people unintentionally, or sometimes I would trigger people into a reaction that I needed to understand or manage. There were days when I was told to just shush and keep my head down and work or to keep the peace, but this went against my soul, my recovery, and my therapy!

Being in Narcissistic abuse recovery, it is part of my recovery to express when I'm feeling triggered, pinpoint what is triggering me and work on it, but also remove myself from the situation or set boundaries. That goes hand in hand with pointing out abusive tactics used by others (knowingly or not) and setting boundaries. I carry this in every sphere I am in. If at work, I notice someone is trying to gaslight me, I will point out the tactic and set a boundary rather than ignoring the abuse happening and sliding it under the rug which would just enable the situation and set a tone for how I will be treated.

Part of who I have become is someone that will stand firm against tactics that have been normalized. My goal is to stand firm to hold people accountable so they may self-reflect and do better and hold my boundaries and allow them to understand why. If they choose not to, that is their prerogative, but at least the individual/groups/environment know where I stand.

Once you find your voice and you are confident in yourself, you don't need validation or confirmation from anyone and you won't mind if people don't like you for your beliefs or opinions because you know yourself, love yourself and trust yourself. And remember, you can only control your delivery, not the reactions of others; that is not yours to own.

Chapter 2

August 31, 10:55 pm

Day trip tomorrow. Somewhere where there is a waterfall. Decided on Tiffany falls near Hamilton. It'll be an extra long day so I'm going to pack food and water for Jazzy and maybe a first aid kit and her booties as well. Maybe a little extra, but you never know. This is going to be good for her; she's been having a rough couple of days since the police let N try to break in and stole *our dog*. She's been sleeping by the door and hasn't eaten in 48 hours. She finally joined me on the couch to sleep today, but I can see how depressed she is.

I had nightmares again last night. I was with him, and he was participating in his first MMA fight and was cheating on me. I was trying to be in his corner to show how loyal I was. I was anxious the entire time and worried he would leave me.

Sometimes I doubt that dreams are your subconscious because there is no way in hell that this is a legitimate worry of mine.

I was contemplating how I would feel if he started dating again and wondering what he would tell another girlfriend about me. This is when I realized that I really wouldn't care about either scenario. Then I wondered how I would feel if he tried to come back as a "treated" man; if he said he was sorry and was working on himself and again, I wouldn't care.

That tells me something.

Of course, I'm still hurt by everything that he did and I'm still learning to cope with and overcome all the trauma, but when it comes to him, I have an understanding that he will never see what he did as wrong because he's a Narcissist and doesn't care and therefore will never actually change. He will always be a pathological liar. He will always be ignorant and racist. So, it all boils down to the fact that, on the inside, he's a terrible person but doesn't see it. He lacks morals and values, and ethics, and that is who he really is. Behind the façade, that is who he really is. I don't want people like that in my life or the life of the people I love. I can't grow with a partner that refuses to embrace growth. I'm not sorry or sad that he is out of my life because his presence was like a poison.

Tonight, I came home from my parent's house, and Allan and Jess were outside having a fire. I left my laundry by the car and joined them for a good part of an hour. It's so nice to have such great neighbours and friends. We have such great conversations. I can't imagine ever having better neighbours. Feel very fortunate to have them next door and very fortunate that N *(or I)* did not tarnish the relationship I have with them. They have been there for me so much more than they realize, and I am so thankful. Their relationship is built on trust and mutual understanding, and shared values, as well as commitment to grow together, and that is what a real relationship should be. What a stark contrast to the one I was in.

Lessons:

- DON'T PLAY SMALL! YOU WERE BORN TO SHINE: It's so wild that as I sit here and reflect, I've had that dream more than once. Each time I could feel the emotions, and I'd wake up in tears and emotionally distraught. The last time I had that dream, I was with Z. I woke up feeling confused as to why I was having a dream like that and why it affected me so much, disgusted with myself for having a dream where I still had feeling for N, guilty that I was having that dream while I was with Z, and maybe this was a sign that I had more work to do. But of course, I have more work to do, I'll always have more work to do. So many lessons to learn from that dream, but the one that stood out was to know your worth and never play small.

I can still see part of the dream in my mind's eye so vividly. The ring, the feeling of anxiety, not wanting to let him out of my sight in case he turned to another woman, feeling like I just desperately wanted to be in his corner and trying to prove how much I could be worth to him and him not even caring. I was just a prop in that dream. A cheerleading, anxiety-ridden prop. I knew what an asset I was, and that I could be helping so many other individuals, but there I was, trying to prove I could be that asset for him. Walking on eggshells to not upset him, rooting him on, and hoping I stay on the team. When really, I'd be better creating my own!

The dream wasn't a reflection of how I felt about my N but rather how I felt about myself. I was making myself small. Putting myself aside to put all my energy into other people. Maybe that is why I had the dream when I was still with Z; I was repeating the same patterns. Trying to prove to someone daily that I was worth loving, that I was in their corner, that I was loyal and always there to support. Same patterns all over again but with a different partner.

The lesson? Don't make yourself small to accommodate anyone. The question is, why are we afraid to shine? Why are we afraid of the thunder we deserve? Why do we think overachieving is a negative quality? Why do we discourage challenging the status quo? Living our genuine and authentic selves? Because we have been taught to play it safe, don't challenge, put our head down and do the work, this is how it's always been done. Don't be different, don't speak up. People are intimidated by confident people. People are intimidated by someone who is comfortable in their own skin. So those people expect us to play small and not rock the boat.

I was once told, at work, that my confidence intimidates people. I internalized that and went home and tried to think of ways to make the less experienced employees at work, more comfortable. Then I thought to myself, "wait… why am I making myself small to accommodate their feelings of inadequacy?" Rather, they should take this opportunity to learn to become more confident. Maybe if they became confident, we'd all work better as a team and we'd then all learn from each other. Playing small doesn't benefit anyone. Not living to your fullest potential doesn't benefit anyone. Rather, it's harmful because you have so much to share and teach!

Do not be afraid to take up space.

Be authentically you.

Your new tribe, the right tribe, will find you; they will be energetically attracted to you and a new journey will begin.

- GROWTH IS UNCOMFORTABLE: Growth takes being uncomfortable, breaking through what you thought was normal, and realizing the opposite may be true, and the need to try that! Growth can be confusing as you are consistently battling what you are conditioned to believe and behave, to how you should/want to start behaving and acting. You are consistently battling yourself and your instincts and what you thought was your intuition. This is exhausting! It takes quite a lot of energy to consistently correct your mind and actions, and reactions.

I always talk about the three phases of a response:

Our first response is what we have been conditioned to feel/think/believe.

Our second response is our correction.

Our third and final response is driven by our new, healing self and the person we want to become.

For example, when I decided to write this book, I initially felt guilty. Worried, scared of what my ex and parents and friends would think. (This guilt-ridden insecurity is my conditioned trauma response).

My second reaction/realization is when I realize that I am working off the old, unhealed, conditioned version of myself.

My third reaction is based on my values and virtues of my healing self. I shouldn't feel bad. I am sharing my story, trying to lead with love and an empathetic heart so others can heal. I am proud and capable of using my voice to bring light to an insidious form of abuse. I should never feel guilty about that; instead, I should be proud of that. And if this triggers anyone, that is a reflection of them and the healing they need to do, rather than a reflection of myself.

- NARCISSISTIC ABUSE ACTUALLY CAUSES BRAIN DAMAGE: What a difficult truth that we all have to come to terms with. As mentioned earlier, being in such a volatile and abusive relationship, you are consistently living in a flight, fight, freeze or fawn state. Your nervous system is always on high alert. This causes an increase in cortisol in your body which wreaks havoc on your nervous system. The Hippocampus, the part of the brain associated mainly with learning and memory, is especially sensitive to the damaging effects of emotional distress, stress, and cortisol. When affected by cortisol, the Hippocampus shrinks. The cortisol also affects the Amygdala, which regulates emotions. So as the Hippocampus is stunted, the Amygdala is stimulated which forces us into more emotional responses and we are then less able to learn or act with our rational mind. When we react off emotion to the insidious abuse from a Narcissist of a toxic person, this is called reactive abuse. The tricky thing about this is that most people who haven't been in this sort of situation do not see the action that caused your reaction, because it is usually very subtle. Instead, they only see your reaction to the subtle abuse.

Personally, I dislike the fact that the term abuse is in the name. Abuse is intentional. It involves a power dynamic and manipulation of that dynamic to oppress, control and hurt. What differentiates reactive "abuse" from abuse is the intent. When you are reacting, or dissociating, you are running off the emotional part of your brain. Due to the constant heightened level of stress and anxiety, you hardly ever get to use the rational part of your brain and are living off volatile emotions as a result of the constant strain. Half the time, you may not remember the things you said or did in reaction to abuse because you have dissociated due to the level of trauma you were experiencing/enduring. Once your nervous system is regulated (by regulated, I mean back to its default, but we all know there is no way to regulate your nervous system if you are always in a heightened state), you have trouble remembering the events, which the Narcissist will then use against you to gaslight you, make you question the events and deflect blame. By the time you realize what is going on, you've gone from describing how their actions made you feel, to fighting over who pays rent, then over how many times s/he has done dishes to the words you are using, and next thing you know, you are apologizing to them.

Does this situation sound familiar?

No, you're not crazy. You're just used to them making you feel like you are.

Are you struggling? 100%. That is not your imagination. Your brain is not unable to reconcile the situation because you have gaps in your memory. Your empathetic guilt-ridden soul has allowed them to convince you that you made a mistake by even approaching whatever your original concern was, and next time, you'll let that behaviour slide avoid the situation because your mind and body literally cannot handle that level of trauma, irrationality and lunacy that comes from their reaction.

For most of my life, the running joke was that I had a poor memory. In grade school, people used to call me "Little Phoebe" after the character Phoebe on the show, Friends. I could sit there, intently listening, and forget the conversation two seconds later. I could remember events my friends and I attended, but only parts of them. I thought this was a trait I got from my mother, the forgetfulness, but it was not a trait she passed down. It was effects of trauma.

It made sense. I don't have a poor memory from genetics. I'm not forgetful because it is a part of who I am but rather, I'm being protected by what my brain perceives as trauma. This caused me to block out and compartmentalize and affected my memory and ability to retain and process information.

I was not crazy.

You are not crazy.

You are not alone.

You are not the only one.

It's not you, it's the trauma.

The goal is to accept who you were, understand who you currently are, and work towards becoming the person you want to be. You can be mad that this happened to you, or you can understand what the trauma has caused and learn to heal, cope, and thrive, and that takes a lot of patience and understanding with yourself. To understand yourself rather than internalizing and blaming yourself or others. As you heal, so will your mind and you can come back from the damage done.

You can't control what has happened to you, but you can control and decide how you move forward.

Chapter 3

September 10, 2:04 am

I began this entry not realizing what time it was, so early in the morning, and my mind is still racing. I'm sure a lot of people could relate. Why is it so hard to shut things off? Or slow it down. I wish there was an easier way for me to record my thoughts. I feel as though the process of writing it down somehow slightly edits what I have to say. I think much faster than I am able to write, and this hinders the translation. Then there's going and finding something to write on or locating your journal, sitting down, and by then, you've passed the moment. I've tried to record, but then I never got around to transcribing.

Well, there's an entry for "thoughts when I'm high," only I'm not high. I was thinking earlier, what is the reason for a life of pain? Is it because for every action, there is a reaction? Cause and effect? Yin and Yang? The balance? Does someone have to hurt someone else to gain? Is this how the universe keeps balance? Or, when it comes to everyone's energies and vibrations, does it matter? Does the universe simply compensate itself if there is hurt in the world and finds its own way to balance? Then what reason for pain? Maybe because pain is the most effective teacher? The most powerful catalyst? But is it though? If it causes damage in the midst? And what is the lesson? How do you know if you've learned the lesson or is life simply a continuous lesson that never ends and is, in itself, the lesson? Small, continued lessons that constantly shape you into the individual that you are meant to become. A person, able to make a difference that is even bigger than the pain of one person. If it heals or makes and molds someone, who may become a person who inspires and encourages many more people. Maybe that person will inspire the next who will inspire someone who cures juvenile diabetes. Is that worth someone's pain? I don't know, but this is the stuff I think about to justify and give a reason for my pain. Even though, compared to many people, my situation would be a dream compared to theirs, and I realize this. But this does not diminish my pain.

Maybe that is my way to cope as well, a way to help me heal.

Switch it up…

Trying to think and send out positivity into this world. Jotting down my thoughts in hopes to be able to speak to the public and help others through my lessons. I mean, it can still be difficult dealing with things out loud, like my hair. I know I want to help people understand but I don't want to talk about it because I am still embarrassed. But this is the exact behaviour that should not be allowed: Inaction.

Inaction cannot be tolerated or accepted. Inaction is the reason for the ignorance that remains and is spread. All those people who are perpetuating the stigmatization of mental illness through inaction. But it also takes being ready. And I'm not. "Wait!" my mind argues. Is that itself inaction? And why am I writing like an ancient philosopher? My argument with myself, should it matter if you are ready? Will I ever be 100 % ready? How can I be honest and speak honestly if I'm pretending to be ready when I'm not? No wonder I never became a judge; this argument with myself is exhausting. Always swaying back and forth like that. Always contemplating and debating with myself.

Time to get some sleep. Real sleep, I hope. Praying for no bad dreams or nightmares tonight.

Lessons:

- EVERYTHING HAPPENS FOR A REASON: Not only does everything happen for a reason, but it will happen in its own diving timing. I know this is going to cause some backlash, and I've thought of it too; does Cancer happen for a reason? Covid? Awful incidents of abuse? But yes, I truly believe it does. Why? Well, I can only speak to my own situation and lessons.

I was speaking with a friend today who told me that she is sorry we lost touch, and she wishes she could have been around back

45

then to protect me. I appreciate the sentiment, and I'm very thankful to have such a wonderful friend in her, but I told her simply that everything that happened genuinely needed to happen.

I truly believe I would not have learned the lessons I needed to learn without being put through that entire situation. There were so many lessons, such as why people don't leave abusive relationships, that I need to learn and not only learn but feel, experience, and overcome in order to truly be able to help people an myself. I now see the lessons that I needed to learn and then learn again, and I know exactly why N was put into my life. There were a number of massive lessons I needed to learn and to learn quickly. I needed to ascend and grow fast to make up for the lessons I've ignored over my lifetime. The pain and resulting lessons were definitely for my benefit rather than my detriment. I just had to get my head out of my butt and look at the long game.

Does it suck that I had to go through that? Those experiences, those relationships? Not just romantic, but friendships and co-workers as well? Yes. Absolutely it sucks! I ran into Narcissists in every area of my life, and not until N, did I really get affected enough to hit rock bottom or understand what I was dealing with. Never would I wish such things on others in order to learn lessons, but my experiences, and an accumulation of experiences from the same kinds of people, forced me down a road I so desperately needed to walk and navigate in order to truly start my healing process and live my soul's purpose. I wouldn't be where I am today if it wasn't for the awful experiences I had or for those awful people in my life. I needed to turn inwards, get help, heal, and understand why I accepted these people in my life. These individuals did not simply impose, I let them in, and I accepted the bare minimum. And N, well, he was the universe's last straw. The one that broke the proverbial camel's back. The last catalyst for lessons I needed to learn before going to the final stage of my journey – finding my authentic self and being comfortable enough in that self to share with the world. To heal in order to help heal.

I truly believe that the universe and Source have a way of maintaining balance. I know I'm going to get some backlash for that, but I truly believe this. Whether it's the healing after trauma or large catastrophic events to shift global consciousness or bring in a surge of empathy that will shift the collective and change the times. It's awful, and I believe that Source, God, whatever you believe in, cries just as we do, but sometimes these awful, tragic, catastrophic situations are what brings the collective together, to rally behind each other for what is right and to be the catalyst for a major shift and movement. For major awakenings, where the collective is forced to grow, evolve, and heal together. The universe gets stagnant too. As a collective, we go through stagnant periods where we start to fall back to the unhealed version collectively. In these moments, the Universe causes collective tower moments just as we have personal tower moments to redirect us and shock us into change and growth.

Hindsight is 20/20. If you try to find the reasons and lessons in things, you can, and you will. Use this to grow, break patterns and generational traumas and forge a new way. For those who do not see a lesson, I feel for you. Maybe you are still hurting and aren't ready to find the lesson in the pain, but there is. They are there. I promise. These lessons are to help us evolve, grow, and reach closer to our fullest potential as humans, as friends and family, and as a community, and then to teach the new generation these lessons so they can do better and make better choices. To lead with love and confidence, not fear, ego or insecurity.

Maybe it's wishful thinking to believe there will be a world of peace, but it's not unreasonable to believe that we can progress with every new lesson and generation, and one day, we will indeed have a majority of people who believe in being kinder and more caring and inclusive and those people will truly speak louder than the rest and move mountains.

- RELEASE THE NEED TO CONTROL THE OUTCOME: A medium once told me there is no such thing as coincidences. Everything happens for a reason. The old me would have thought, "oh yeah?? So does Cancer happen for a reason?" but instead, I understood what that meant, and I agreed with her. Synchronicity, Universal, and Angel guidance.

The moment I stopped trying to guide or control the outcome, started listening to my angels and letting the universe and Source guide me, things started falling into place. And the moment I stopped, the moment I got too busy to invest in myself, I stopped listening to my intuition, things started to fall apart. This is the lesson that I had to learn and relearn over and over. The toxic patterns I had to overcome.

So often, because I always felt so starved for love, needed validation and had this anxious attachment style, I was prone to relationships built on trauma bonds and a lack of sense of self. I would throw myself into every relationship and put everything into my partner and his efforts and endeavors. With the past two partners, N included, I worked jobs I hated so I could make myself available to my partner. I would support their dreams before exploring my own passions. Take N, for example. He wanted a new start, his own business, so I helped him create it. I did the accounting, I did the invoicing, found him an accountant, kept his books in line, did anything and everything he needed. Imagine I took that effort and that energy and put it into myself. I'd be uber-successful! Then the ball dropped, I moved on and I found my person and did the same thing. Invested fully in him and worked jobs that got me by but mainly allowed me to work around his schedule. I made sure I was available to him. Then I found work that I loved, but again, I took a position that allowed me to be available in case he needed help.

Every hour of my day that I wasn't doing my job, I was working for him. The moment he would send me a text me to do something, I'd find a spare moment at work to find a computer, log onto the internet quickly and make the fix or change. When I worked from home, I spent all my breaks and my time after work doing work for his business. Again, I invested everything into helping him and left my endeavours to the side. I was too tired to work on my own goals and passions after work and after helping him. My brain was too tired for things I loved like reading, volunteering (which also meant I was unavailable to help him which was unacceptable to me). I started this book in 2020, and here we are in 2023, and I'm finally going through with my dream.

Again, there were lessons I needed to learn; I had patterns I needed to break. I needed to find the time, courage, and discipline to invest into myself! Find the strength to believe in myself as much as I believe in them. Make it a priority to make time for myself just as much as I did them. Work as hard for myself as I did for them and others. When I was too busy for myself, when I was giving myself to everyone else and not reinvesting in myself, I was essentially lowering my vibrations. I was telling the Universe, I didn't value myself or any of the wonderful gifts I had been rewarded. I didn't appreciate, value, or put in place the growth and lessons I had learned in such hard ways. I had to stop, pause, think, reflect, and get back to my roots. Work on me and my energy. Raise my vibrations by healing and work to stay there. Put myself first. I needed to journal, meditate, connect with nature, and allow myself downtime to process. All these important outlets. When I wasn't doing these things, I was attracting what I was projecting, and I was projecting stressful, tired, exhausted, negative, reactive energy. It was time to stop living for others and truly live for myself.

- FOCUS ON YOURSELF: Self-love and self-care are not selfish but necessary. You cannot pour from an empty cup, and you cannot give what you don't have. I lost myself when I was giving myself to everyone and everything and leaving nothing for myself. I was focused on building my partner's business, on my work and employer, on my relationship, and on my parents, but not on myself. I was spreading myself thin and leaving no room to refill my own cup. That is precisely when the universe will start teaching you some hard lessons, and you'll find yourself repeating some painful patterns. We are not meant to focus all our attention outward and neglect ourselves. Put yourself first and discover what you need to be the best version of yourself. If you don't know what that is, then it's time to explore and figure that out. What are some things you used to love but lost the passion? What are things you enjoyed doing but would never do alone? Time to love doing things with only yourself. Go to the movies, go to the park and feed the animals, go to a restaurant alone or take a trip alone. Fall back in love with yourself and rediscover yourself!

- STIGMAS ARE ALIVE AND REAL: I wrote these journal entries during a time when I was taking 2mg of Lorazepam daily. Lorazepam is from the Benzodiazepine family. It works by slowing brain activity to all for relaxation. It's basically a sedative used to treat anxiety and insomnia caused by anxiety or stress (Medlineplus.gov). In my case, the stress from the incidents (the relationship with N, the traumatic arguments, the abuse, the confinement, our dog…) caused me so much trauma that I couldn't sleep, and when I could, I had awful nightmares. I tried everything, and nothing was helping the anxiety. The fear of even taking my dog for a walk down the street, the fear of going to the grocery store, making sure 3 or 4 times before retiring that all the doors and windows were locked kept me paralyzed. I checked the parking lot from my window, made sure my motion camera was set and angled properly, made sure the air conditioner was bolted in, and the windows secured. It crippled me. The stress was real.

I spoke wit my doctor and she prescribed me Lorazepam. I started low and ended up needing 2mg a day, which is the high dose and the maximum. Lorazepam is also highly addictive, and the side effects include drowsiness, dizziness, tiredness, weakness, unsteadiness, diarrhea, nausea, changes in appetite, restlessness or excitement, constipation, blurred vision, and changes in sex drive or ability. Major side effects include shuffling walk, persistent fine tremors or inability to sit still, and trouble talking. Rash-like hives/itching, swelling of the face, eyes, or mouth. Wheezing; or shortness of breath. Yellowing of skin or eyes and, of course, irregular heartbeat. A great goody bag of surprises. Of course, these are just possible side effects, and I didn't experience them all, but it's worth noting how prescribed and normalized pharmaceuticals can alter or hinder your abilities. I want you to think about this as we continue this discussion.

Lorazepam was numbing. I would sit there in a haze for an entire movie and not even realize the movie has ended. When I finally saw the credits going up, I would think to myself, "over already? How did I miss the majority of the movie?". I took the RX a few hours before bed, so it's not like I was taking them first thing in the morning and trying to function during the day.

The Lorazepam helped me sleep, but it never felt restful. I stopped having nightmares, but only because I basically stopped dreaming. I'd have a dream here and there, but I wouldn't remember any of them, just the feeling that I had a dream that night. It was such an awkward, out-of-body feeling. Like I was present but felt zero emotion, no drive, and no motivation. I could go the entire day without eating or drinking, which didn't help the stomach and gastro issues I experienced from the drug and stress. It was difficult to eat anything because I immediately had an upset stomach, or it would go right through me like a bad takeout filled with MSG, only it was everything I ate!

I couldn't live that way. I couldn't even retain anything that I was reading. I didn't have any motivation to see anyone. I couldn't function. So, I gave up the Lorazepam and stuck to Cannabis only. Sativa hybrid during the day and Indica at night.

I slowly started to dream again. I had an appetite, my stomach was still a wreck, but that's what trauma and anxiety can do. I felt like doing things, going out, and enjoying the sunshine. I started having ideas which meant motivation and inspiration! I was wild! Cannabis got me to function and got me out of the fog. I started to work out again. I went on hikes every weekend with Jazzy, I went on road trips, and I hung out with people. Reintroduced myself slowly to the outside world. Yet I was still embarrassed to share with people that I smoked Cannabis. I didn't want people to know because what would they think? People would judge me, look at me like a stoner, like I'm always high just sitting on my couch watching South Park and eating junk food. Yet I was the total opposite! I was functional and productive, finding myself through inspiration and motivation.

Therein lies the irony. To tell people I had prescribed Lorazepam and taking the max dose was totally fine. Perfectly understandable. Could it alter my perception? Impede my ability to make sound decisions or function in a normal fashion? Yes, absolutely! I should never be allowed to drive while prescribed and taking Lorazepam. Yet Cannabis had such a negative stigma even

51

though it's legalized just like Lorazepam. Isn't it ironic that we normalize taking some drugs that cause so much more harm to an individual? Today, if I were to go to work while taking Lorazepam, no one would call HR. But if I were to smoke some Sativa and head to work, I'd get fired. Going to work intoxicated and under the influence of substances.

Only this year, 2023, have I become more comfortable with sharing that I smoke Cannabis. Even now, I feel insecure sharing that information because I don't want people to judge me. This is a conditioned view and reaction. Conditioned by a society that historically has tried to control the narrative around Cannabis and Cannabis users. From the initial war on drugs that tried to demonize Black people in the Jazz industry to associating Cannabis with the Mexican community and trying to alienate them, all the while benefitting from the industry in alternative ways. The culture created surrounding Cannabis was never a matter of the substance being an issue but rather using the substance to paint communities as problematic. And here we stand in 2023, still slightly ashamed to share that I smoke Cannabis because of the stigma associated and fear of judgment.

We are now in an era where we can recreate, redefine, and correct old narratives that conditioned societal views. Societal norms are all created by the Patriarchy, but norms, symbolism, and language are all fluid! Everything evolves. It's up to us to direct the evolution. What do we want? What kind of world do we want to live in? These norms, these stereotypes, and stigmas are created by people and can be changed by people. We are not locked into the previous generation's way of thinking, and we do not need to perpetuate their traumas or ignorance. This is our time to shine and recreate a world and humanity in a way that leads with love and not ego.

Chapter 4

September 17th, 8:55 pm-ish

Procrastinating because I have to read this interview transcript from the video interview with the detective. Really not looking forward to this. Putting on Forged in Fire so that I can have something playing in the background, not just pure and daunting silence.

The sound of the hammer hitting the steel makes me somehow feel strong. Or more like I associate it with strength. That is powerful and encouraging almost. That's the word I was looking for, semantics. How important. I was just looking down at the remote in my hands, typing in the search and the transcript underneath, and thought to myself, "This would be a photo representation of my life in my scrapbook of life if I had one". That picture right there would be a photo I would take if I could simply blink my eyes, have my mind store it in my life's timeline. Imagine what it would be like if it were possible, almost like a sci-fi movie, where a person can download their timeline onto a USB or chip and then watch it. Play it back. A highly curated digital scrapbook of photos that depict or represent very significant moments in your life. Moments that molded you and shaped you. A slideshow you could play at your wedding, a timeline of moments that illustrate your relationship from your vantage point.

This snapshot of the transcript under the remote would be one of those snapshots for me. It would be one of those snapshots with such complex meaning. The hands, holding the remote clearly a way to procrastinate. The transcript that is the second place task, the one being avoided. She is turning on the TV because she is procrastinating; avoiding. Another might view that photo differently. She may be turning on the TV not as a distraction but rather as background noise as she reads through this transcript. Like white noise students need to focus when studying.

One photo can be interpreted in so many ways. The TV helps me focus. The sound of the hammer hitting steel makes me feel strong and like reading this transcript cannot hurt me. Subconsciously helping to ease my anxiety. But yes, I am also procrastinating. This is very clear since I am currently writing rather than reading this dreaded transcript. I could easily say that I have been meaning to write more anyways, but the fact that I decided to do this right before reading the transcript is clearly a sign of avoidance rather than following through with a goal. At least I can recognize this.

It's very difficult to get myself to do anything related to this court case. I avoid, redirect, forget, even though it's on my mind all the time. I don't use PTSD/c-PTSD as an excuse though I could. I know that healing is my responsibility, and taking control of the situation is also my responsibility. I need to be able to recognize the behaviours that are associated with PTSD/c-PTSD, process them, and address them so that I can heal, manage, break patterns. Healing is not easy. Unravelling and unpacking years of trauma and learning to cope and live with the damage is a daily battle but one that will make me a stronger, more understanding individual with lessons I can hopefully pass on to others.

Lessons:

- HEAL IN YOUR OWN WAY: This entry makes me feel sad but also, gives me a sense of understanding. When I wrote this, I associated all those outcomes with PTSD/c-PTSD. And yes, as mentioned before, both cause brain damage and do guide actions and thoughts but are never an excuse.

Ironically, scrolling through TikTok, thanks to rolling Covid lockdowns, I realized just how many people struggle with the same afflictions. I never understood that this could be anything other than anxiety until TikTok. I learned a lot about c-PTSD which can also mimic ADHD or being on the spectrum. Everything started to click and make sense. I started to be able to connect the dots and really understand myself.

Here I am, 38, and still trying to treat anxiety/OCD, which I was diagnosed with at 13. But what if that's not it, but those things are a by-product of c-PTSD?! Mind-blowing! It all starts to make sense! I've been treating the symptoms but not addressing the root cause. I'm here thinking that my anxiety stems from my genetics (in a sense, it does), as well as my other symptoms, like hair pulling, skin picking, and stimming. My life finally made sense! I wasn't alone!

The irony of this entire situation is that when I started my healing journey, a good friend got mad at me and actually stopped associating with me because she believed I needed to heal in silence. Rather than talk about and post about my traumas and share my healing journey, she told me I should delete social media. She asked me out for coffee, strictly to have that conversation with me. Looking back now, I think my content triggered her because she may have seen a lot of herself in it, which isn't my issue; it's hers. But I digress. Everyone and their mother are going to have an opinion on how you should heal, silently is usually the suggestion. But if you want to heal out loud, you go ahead and you do that. If you want to share on social media, you go ahead and you do that. If you want to find your own way, you go ahead and you do that.

If I had listened to my former friend, I wouldn't have healed as much as I did and as quickly as I did. I wouldn't have made the connections that were instrumental in my healing journey and recovery, and I definitely wouldn't have found my passion and my calling. I'd still be in the same pattern of hiding, shame, loneliness, and isolation. Social media played a crucial role in my recovery. Sharing my story and having others tell me they related and went through the same, talked about processing emotions, the outcome, the aftermath, and the shared experiences helped me heal. I followed therapists and survivors. I followed motivational pages, informative pages, and I learned, soaked up all the information, and that was, as I mentioned, instrumental in my healing journey. Even my therapist told me she'd never seen someone do as much work on myself and grow as quickly as I did, and I have social media to (partially) thank for that. Not a single person agreed with me healing out loud, but I did it anyways, and I am here now as a result.

Your healing journey is yours and yours alone. Everyone is always going to have something to say, or some sort of opinion or two cents on your journey, but this is not their journey. They have never walked your path, been in your shoes, or experienced your pain, your trauma, your isolation and disconnect. They can give you all the solicited or unsolicited advice they want, but in the end, you are the only one that must live with, and take accountability for the consequences of your actions, inactions, healing, or lack thereof.

I still have a long way to go before I can rid myself of the conditioned norms. Don't get me wrong, I'm about prescription drugs as needed. I studied Big Pharma in university and though I know the benefits of pharmaceuticals, I also understand the potential harm and that we live in a Capitalist society.

I still have a long way to go myself so that I may live my most authentic self without any feeling of shame or guilt. No one is perfect, and it's easy to forget that healing is a journey, and with each evolution of yourself, you get a little bit closer to the most natural, authentic, comfortable, and genuine version of yourself. Even as you make progress, you must stay strong and disciplined to maintain that progress instead of reverting back to the unhealed version of yourself that sabotages your success. Don't be so focused on the outcome that you miss the beauty of the process.

- PATIENCE IS KEY: Patience with others, but most importantly, patience with yourself. To the above point, even after writing the book, it took me over 3 years to start editing and finishing it. I had it open. I had every intention, every want, and desire, but I kept procrastinating. Other priorities. Again, I was putting myself and my own goals on the back burner, but everything has its purpose.

Years later, I finally decided to finish editing and while going through my 3rd review, I realized I had grown so much since my 2nd edit, and I have more things I want to say. Some things evolved as I learned more, which changed how I feel and how I view the situations and the lessons. I felt slightly ashamed for some of the lessons I initially attributed to the entry, but I realized that I was still in the beginning stages of my healing journey and needed to be patient with myself as lessons will always evolve with new perspectives. I was evolving, learning, growing and still filled with hurt. I'm proud of the evolution that came as a result of much needed reflection.

- BE KIND TO YOURSELF: Brené Brown (if you haven't read "Daring Greatly" you haven't lived) explains the difference between shame and guilt. Guilt, as she puts it, is adaptive and helpful. It forces us to feel something we've done, which makes us hold up our values against the feelings of psychological discomfort (BrenéBrown.com). It can be a catalyst, a motivator, and a seed of inspiration. Shame, on the other hand, is painful and makes us feel as though we are inadequate or flawed. It is detrimental to our development, our sense of belonging and our sense of worthiness, which is important to understanding love and unconditional love vs. conditional love. Shame distorts our sense of self, whereas guilt can help build our resilience and shapes our moral compass and sense of self.

Another way to explain it is as follows: when a child spills a cup of milk because s/he was running around too quickly with a full glass in hand. Notice the difference in reactions:

Shame: You're bad for spilling the milk.

Guilt: Running through the house was careless, which made you spill the milk.

Shame: You are associating the incident with the child. The child is not bad. The child did a "bad thing" by spilling the milk.

Guilt: The child knew s/he shouldn't run because it's careless and result in a mess. The child is good but made a mistake which resulted in spilling the milk.

Acknowledging this difference is the first step to changing how you view yourself and by extension, speak to yourself. This is crucial to growth and giving ourselves the grace to make mistakes as we grow. We must learn to be kind to ourselves, always. Hold ourselves accountable, of course, but be kind. For instance, you are unpacking your groceries and you drop the eggs on the floor. What is your first reaction?

Is it:

A) I'm so stupid!
B) Well, that was a careless mistake. I should slow down. (And all this is done without any name-calling or deflating of your self-worth).

Most people's first reaction is option A. Without even realizing it, we demonize ourselves for the smallest mistakes. We internalize the mistake with the language we use, and whether you realize it or not, this is what you are programming into your inner child and subconscious mind every single time. This is the version of you that has conditioned you to associate making mistakes as being bad, and then needing to redeem yourself to regain affection. Thereby creating an anxious attachment style. There is a need for validation and redemption, and love is viewed as conditional, and something earned but easily lost as a result. Even with yourself and self-love. Continuous negative self-talk can cause an individual to only feel good about themselves when they are doing something good or being productive or shining bright. But what happens when that person/you loses gas? Burns out? Or when life changes and priorities need to shift, and you aren't able to do those things that make you consistently feel like a winner? In those downtimes, you get really down. You beat yourself up for being "lazy". But you're not lazy. You're just not used to balance. You're not used to loving yourself, let alone loving yourself when you aren't doing something that you deem qualifies as a task that earns love and praise. Such as sitting on the couch, not working, reading a book, or sleeping in.

It is crucial that we learn to speak more kindly to ourselves, have more patience with ourselves, and give ourselves a little more grace. All the patience, gratitude, kindness, and encouragement you would give to others, it's time to turn back into yourself. Turn that inward and give yourself just as much kindness and grace, and patience you would anyone else. You deserve it just as much if not more!

Chapter 5

Sept 28, 8:19 pm

A friend of mine is upset with me for something that is beyond my control and for being inconvenienced. For… being… inconvenienced. For offering to do something for me and then getting upset for having to go through with it. This friend is also upset because I didn't mention she was going to get a letter that would explain her having to keep her offer in a situation. I wanted to tell her. I know, I know, I should have told her. I wanted to sit down with her for coffee and explain, but she seemed to be avoiding me. Maybe she was. Maybe she just didn't get back to me because she was busy. Who knows?

Maybe I made a bigger deal out of the situation than I needed to. But the point is, that is how I deal with things that stress me out. I'd rather have a sit-down face-to-face than send a text regarding something that is important to me. I ran the situation over and over in my head; "Just text her. Why do you feel like you need to sit down and talk?" Then it dawned on me. It's because of her patterns, how she's reacted in the past. This was my way of dealing with the anxiety, have a face-to-face talk and not over text.

Maybe she'd see how sincerely sorry I was for the inconvenience. Maybe she'd see how inconvenienced we all are. We are all in the same boat here and lets all support each other. One day turned into the next and then the next and then the next and I kept telling myself "I'll text her tomorrow…" then the next day came and my anxiety about her reaction would build, and I'd put it off then my anxiety would build, and I'd put it off and next thing you know she received the request, and she texts me furious.

I blame myself. I literally cannot count the number of times I have cried over this. I regret all of this. I regret calling her that night. I regret calling the police. I regret everything. None of this would be happening if I had just done nothing.

I wouldn't be bald from stress right now.

I wouldn't have lost half my friends.

I wouldn't be so depressed and anxious and suffering from PTSD daily.

I wouldn't have had my dog stolen.

Maybe if he had sobered up that night, if I had just let the commotion and abuse subside and rode it out, he would realize what he had done and decided living together is not a good option and would have finally just moved out on his own. I regret everything.

Sometimes I'm so depressed that I think about ending it. It has crossed my mind more often than not. I just hate living this life so much. And what good do I do anyways? I'm a lousy friend, apparently. I don't get to see my nieces and nephews as much as I'd like, or at all anymore, since my toxic relationship ruined friendships. I love those kids, but I just can't even get myself to want to leave the house to visit. I just stay home with Jazzy where I can sit alone and feel safe but insane in this mind riddled with fear, anxiety, stress, trauma, mistakes made and regrets.

My nights are literally just watching TV and my mind going a million miles a minute, and even though I know I should do something to change that, go out, visit a friend, do anything! I don't. I can't. I'm frozen. I don't volunteer like I used to. I give no value to anyone's life. I've never struggled this much in my mind.

In university, I had a goal. I had classes to attend and grades to make. While I was so depressed, I had a purpose. A goal. A path. Do this to get better. Do this to be better. Do this to give Jazzy and *our dog* better.

Now I look at me, and I'm disappointed. I work a job that makes me so replaceable. I don't even help save animals anymore. I literally have no purpose. I'm so conflicted. All this because I called the police that night. All this feeling, the depression, the trauma, the anxiety, the heartache, the seclusion and fear and nightmares. No sleep. No appetite. I force myself to eat daily. I force myself to gain weight after losing so much. The stress is eating at me from the inside out.

What good has come out of this? I worry for the future because of all of this. I stress because of all of this. I'm bald because of all of this. I just can't. I don't want to deal. So, I avoid. And that hurts other people. This trauma, this anxiety is ruining my life and I don't know how to control it. I worry that I may never be able to control it. It scares me. Where does that leave me? As a shitty friend? A troublesome daughter? A crappy Aunt? What purpose does my life have after all that? I'm not even a great employee... always missing work, crying at work, unable to focus and do my job. So, what am I really doing here?

You ever wonder, "who would come to my funeral? Who would care? What would they say about the life I lived?".

What would they say about me? Was I absent? Troubled? Dramatic? Would my nieces and nephews miss me? Be sad? Remember me? That breaks me. Who would know or understand why I never called or visited? Who would know my story? Who would know what was going on in my head? In my mind?

Worrying

Thinking

Regretting

Crying

Thinking

Worrying

This cycle.

I hate this struggle in my mind. And I must live like this, everyday, in my mind.

Lessons

- LEARN TO SIT WITH YOURSELF: Such an easy concept but so difficult to do. It takes practice to be truly present and ok with being in your own mind. Our minds are so powerful and shape how much we do or don't love ourselves. But learning to sit with yourself and enjoy your own company is a gift most people struggle to master, and this is where we learn the greatest lessons.

Being present and being able to sit with my own mind didn't come easily to me. By yourself in your thoughts can be a very dangerous place. I tried to be able to quiet my mind so I could sit with myself. I've tried meditating, but it truly was difficult. I did guided meditations, but my mind would still wander, and I gave up, thinking I was just not good at it because I wasn't! It can be very frustrating to know that you need to learn this skill that is crucial for your evolution and growth, and you simply can't (enter negative self talk). Then I realized, it's not that I'm bad at it, it's that I:

1. Don't practice.
2. Haven't found the right method for me.

I loved Yoga, but my mind would still wander. Hikes in nature, mind still wandered. Knitting, still wandered. Reading, STILL WANDERED! I knew I had to learn to sit with myself and be comfortable with that, but how can I do that when I can't find a moment to quiet my mind?

Then one day, as I was doing the dishes, I realized; I was present. Not a single thought, not a single worry. I was simply going through the motions of the dishes, mind completely blank. That was my method! Yeah, late in the game, but better to figure it out late than never! When we went to look at our house, it was everything I ever wanted! The floor plan I wanted, the design I wanted, and it also had my dream garden! It had every flower on my wish list! Poppies, Tulips, Peonies, Hostas and Hydrangeas! It was like the Universe read my mind! I could spend forever watering and looking at my garden and I realized that watering my garden was a great way for me to meditate. I almost feel like the water moving side to side was a form of EMDR (the very cheap version) and helped me zone out and be present. Perfect!

Now that I knew I could meditate and what I needed in order to meditate (some sort of repetitive motion that requires attention but not too much), I was able to sit with myself for short periods of time. From there, I was able to learn how to consciously quiet my mind so I could sit with myself in my own quiet company.

I truly started to enjoy my own company. Though sometimes difficult, I learned to sit with myself and reflect without getting anxious or depressed. I thought about my role in my current relationship and my past relationships. Not just with romantic partners but with friends and family as well. I thought about how much I enabled, allowing the bar to be set so low and accepting what I contributed to the situation. I reflected on my traumas. I tried to follow that rabbit hole to find the very root of the issue. I looked at my reactions and triggers and worked on those.

Learning to sit with myself, and quiet my mind was crucial to my healing process. It allowed me the space to self-reflect and analyze in a calmer state with a clearer mind. It also allowed me to learn how to be in the moment. How to listen more actively and be more patient. Turning inwards were where the "AH HA!" moments happened that allowed me to see my traumas, the roots, and address them.

It turns out, it wasn't that I wasn't good at meditating, I just hadn't found the right method. And to that point, if you are trying, and you find your mind wandering, that's ok! Notice and acknowledge that your mind wandered and bring it back. The more you do this, and the more you practice, the better you will get!

- DON'T SHOULDER ALL THE BLAME: This is a trauma response, and again, I see such an unhealed version of myself here, in this journal entry, attached to another Narcissist. This right here is a testament to how unhealed I was and how long that stemmed. I have surrounded my inner most relationships with Narcissists. From my best friend in high school to friends in adulthood, to my partners. The patterns were staggering. And let us assess the red flags in that journal entry as a great segway into my next point: Surround yourself with people who have the ability to self-reflect.

Now, let's dissect my trauma here and address some very valuable points.

1. People's actions and emotions are theirs and theirs alone. You cannot control their reactions, only your delivery. Here we can dissect the red flags in the friend's behaviour.
2. The only person your paralyzing anxiety is hurting is yourself. Here we will dissect the red flags in my own behaviour.

First, we need to remind ourselves that the way people receive messages depends on their circumstances, trauma, lenses, and ability to self-reflect. The way another perceives your message, tone, and intent has nothing to do with your message but rather the insecurity or trauma mirrored back to the individual that triggers something in them, some trauma that must be healed. When people react or are reactive to a message, generally speaking, the issue is not the message or the person delivering it but rather their own personal issues or trauma driving a trigger that influences their reaction or perception. Usually, these are the people that will be thinking of an answer or a response even before you are able to finish what you are saying. They aren't interested in listening but rather in proving their own point of view. They are bent on misunderstanding you or hyper focusing on either a sentence, a word, or the tone of your voice. All toxic behaviours, all ways to manipulate and redirect the conversation. Truthfully, there is no sense in trying to explain, re-explain, try to explain in another manner. You end trying to correct their perception for whatever they are hyper-fixated on and before you know it, you are way past in left field and have forgotten what the initial discussion was about, and you can't understand how it got there. To argue with someone who doesn't want to listen, is in itself, irrational.

People who are more likely to respond are those who are able to listen actively and be present in the moment. Those who are able to self-reflect and understand themselves and they're in the situation. These people are more likely to want to engage in solution-based discussions rather than problem-based arguments. I'm sure you're familiar with these kinds of people; solution-based individuals identify the issue and brainstorm ways to actively work towards a resolution. People who are problem-based are the kinds of people that have an issue for every solution you offer, or in cases of discussion, they are more likely to be fixed on all the things wrong and all the mistakes rather than understand mistakes were made and move forward towards a resolution. It can be severely draining talking to someone that is problem based. Someone that keeps redirecting the issue to the problem when you have mentioned 5 or six times a plan to move forward. These are the people with whom you who have to learn to take your energy back from and move forward without them. It's unfortunate, but your energy is sacred. It's your life force, and people who drain you will not only drain you mentally but energetically as well and by extension, emotionally and physically. You'll have less to give to the people who deserve it as you're expending so much on the people that don't.

- COMMUNICATION IS A TWO-WAY STREET: Above, we talked about how people receive messages and what trauma they may attach to their interpretation. Now it's time to do some self-reflection on yourself. How do you receive information? What trauma are you possibly bringing to the table? What is triggering you, and what is the deeper root cause of that trigger? What is being reflected to you, that you are not a fan of? What is making you defensive? There are so many layers to consider, but we all receive information through some sort of veil. Conditioning, trauma, societal norms, cultural norms; no one is free from the veil. This will also determine how we express ourselves and respond to people. Are we reacting or responding? And when responding, what is our intent?

I am a firm believer that the intent should always be to help, not to hurt. Of course, we never intentionally want to hurt (generalized statement but I imagine the individuals reading this book are good people, not more Narcissists), but sometimes we react out of anger or trauma, or we unintentionally cause harm by not being aware of what we say, how we say it, or who we say it to. It is so important to understand intent vs. impact when delivering messages and take a moment to think about what you want to say before you say it. And if you are too triggered, pause, and come back at another time. That's ok too.

We all have examples of reactions that hurt, when the reaction is defensive and people become belittling or insulting whether on purpose or not. Whether because they are having a trauma response, are mean spirited, or whatever the case may be. Then there are the more subtle responses or statements where the intent isn't to hurt, but the impact is harmful.
For instance, when someone asks a woman "When are you going to have kids?". This happens to me more often than I can count. The issue is, what if that woman is trying to have a baby and just experienced a miscarriage? Or if that person is unable to bear children and has been trying and has been unsuccessful? What if that woman has a hysterectomy for a medical reason and is not able to carry a child on her own but would do anything for that opportunity? Or what if this is a woman that doesn't want children and wants to focus on herself? Or a woman healing and unable to dedicate herself to that kind of responsibility right now or ever. Or someone working hard with their partner every day in order to be able to afford a child and are struggling to get there in today's economy? Your question is seemingly innocent and genuinely comes with good intentions, but the impact can be harmful.

Does it take work to be self-aware? Yes, of course it does. And it also takes a willingness to understand how you affect others. It takes practice, as does anything else in life. The question is, how badly do you want to be a better and more evolved version of yourself? One that is able to live in peace, able to manage your triggers and navigate the world with love rather than anger, ego and resentment? Staying in a lower vibration is easy; it really takes nothing at all. Negative energy is a contagion; infectious, and easier to stay in. Being in a high vibration, a vibration of healing and love takes work and needs to be maintained, but the wisdom, confidence, self-assuredness, and happiness that comes with it is worth it.

- SURROUND YOURSELF WITH PEOPLE WHO CAN SELF-REFLECT: Don't kid yourself. Self-reflection is hard and is a skill that needs to be practiced. The added challenge is when your responses are related to triggers. It is very difficult to self-reflect if you are worked up and seeing things through an angry lens. Just as it is important to be able to regulate your emotions after a situation, it is crucial to take a moment to revisit the situation after the fact and talk yourself through it and through how you're feeling, what you contributed to the situation and what pivot points or steps could have been taken for a more peaceful outcome? What did you do and what could you have done better?

There are many ways in which people run from issues, but I'll share my experience in this situation. The unhealed, or lesser healed version of myself was always quite reactive and defensive in situations, and rather than go home and think about the situation, that person would find every reason to justify her actions. That girl led with ego, not with a healing, empathetic heart. That girl was filled with hurt, consumed with a need to be heard, the endless search for validation and led with her trauma. In that heightened and insecure state, everything triggers you. And when that girl was alone, in her room, finally able to think and feel, she was hyperemotional with no one but her unhealed mind to guide her through the situation.

The version of myself today works very hard to get better at self-reflecting. We touched on the types of responses above; the conditioned response, then the moment of reflection, then the response in line with the person you are trying to become. This tiny moment of self-reflection can be built on. Self-reflection leads to a better sense of self and stronger values. It helps build better relationships and communication as well as opinions and views on anything and everything. It won't always be easy, and it won't always be fun times and good conversations with yourself. Especially if you have a guilty conscience and you're a people pleaser. But it will make you a better version of yourself. It helped me in all areas of my life and keeps me in line and in tune with my soul's purpose and it will help you do the same.

Surround yourself with these kinds of people. The self-reflective ones. These people are more likely to be in line with you, your energy, and your vibration. These people are less likely to trigger you, make you reactive, and revert back to the unhealed

68

version of yourself. And if they do, as is likely, they will be more apt to helping you through your triggers, rather and fuelling your fire. Your energy is precious, and the more you pour it into the people who make you reactive and keep you reactive, the less energy you have to spend on people or things that feed and nourish your soul. This doesn't mean that you have to eject people from your life, but you definitely have to set boundaries and change your expectations of them. You can't move to another evolution of yourself if you hold onto things that are not allowed, or not meant to come with you. You have to let those things go with grace so you can move forward, and hopefully, watching you shine will inspire them to do their own work.

This is a difficult and lonely process. This is the part of the glow up no one talks about. Remember, not everyone is meant to be with you for your entire journey, and that's OK. If they cannot meet you at our level, your new evolved version of yourself, set those boundaries. Let them go with love. If they grow, and are able to catch up, amazing! If they don't that's not yours to bear. Never play small to accommodate anyone. You were born to shine!

- REFLECT TO REMIND YOURSELF HOW FAR YOU'VE COME: Looking back at this entry, I am taken aback by the guilt I felt for calling the police. For thinking the entire situation was my fault, as if I orchestrated the entire thing with the purpose of inconveniencing people. It shocks me to read that I would have done things differently, that my boundaries were so loose, that I couldn't see the red flags, that I didn't see the patterns, that I was still shocked even though I knew what the likely result would be and how frozen the thought made me.

It truly shows me how deeply ingrained my trauma was and how distorting it can be, being subjected such abuse for long. How much it can mess with your mind. I was looking back at photos from the early years, then I looked at photos of me in the latter years, and I saw how much weight I had lost during that time. How unhealthy my hair looked (and I was losing it by then, too). How grey my skin was and how dark under my eyes were. Granted, they always are, but I looked at my passport photo, which I took with makeup on, and lord almighty, I truly looked sick. The trauma from all the years, the stress and the heightened nervous state, had made me mentally and physically ill. I had been in the mental health ward, I had nervous breakdowns, I was sick all the time, sick to my stomach, I had no energy no matter how much I slept, and I had awful sleep when I did sleep. It is truly a testament to what awful things that kind of energy-draining, insidious, long-term abuse can do to a person's body.

I also have to own the pain, own the entry. I have to own the shame that comes with that entry; with letting people in, and seeing my vulnerability, hurt and defeat. I have to go back and revisit, so I can understand, forgive myself and move forward. That journey is painful; it never is going to be without any pain, but it helps me appreciate myself and ground myself when I feel like I'm not winning. When I feel overwhelmed and like I'm being lazy or being unproductive or losing motivation, I think back to who I was, that person, that hurt, pained, and damaged person, and the person I am now. I count the lessons and I count the small wins. In this, I can appreciate the journey and the present moment rather than being anxious that I'm not where I want to be. Because in essence, when I am down, lazy, and unmotivated, it's because I'm overwhelmed and anxious. Whether it's due to my own energy, the energy of the people around me or the world as a collective consciousness. I have to take a moment to ground myself so I can come back to my feelings, my true self, rid myself of the energies or the chords of others and that's when I will find my pride and confidence again. This is also an important lesson; you won't always be on the up and up. It's essential to feel, process and regain the strength to move up again. It's ok to take two steps backwards but learn from it.

- THE EMPATH AND THE NARCISSIST: Here it comes. I bet you all have been wondering when I was going to touch on this, weren't you? The Empath and the Narcissist. The usual codependent relationship. Why is this? Why does it always seem like an Empath gets stuck with a Narcissist?

First, I want to explain that this is not always the case and saying "always" is a gross generalization. Often, a Narcissist will align themselves with an Empath, but that doesn't mean always. I have seen Narcissists in relationships with other Narcissists who then raised an Empathic child. The world is wild like that, but I digress.

So why do we, as Empaths, seem to attract Narcissists? Or rather, accept Narcissists. Each situation and relationship is personal, but often, a Narcissist will align themselves with an Empath because we are healers, usually have some traumas we are bearing, we want to see the best in everyone, we have loose boundaries, and most importantly, we will use empathy to excuse many behaviours that others wouldn't. This allows the Narcissist to behave badly longer than s/he would be able to with another individual. As Empaths, we tend to over-empathize with Narcissists; we understand their trauma, we feel their reasoning, we can sympathize with the coping mechanisms, and because we internalize, we rationalize.

The tricky thing is that there is a second layer to that. The lack of boundaries due to our trauma that can cause an anxious or avoidant attachment style and a need for validation. Granted, not every Empath has an anxious or avoidant attachment style or unhealed trauma. But if you've been sucked in and tied in by a Narcissist, chances are you have some sort of unhealthy attachment style and a need for validation. This is why the first few times the Narcissist does something hurtful, they play the trauma card & they play to the Empath's heartstrings. Then the Empath forgives, the Narcissist love bombs, and then the relationship resumes. Done, they've got you. With every new discretion, the Narcissist will take advantage of your empathetic and nurturing heart, and they will ask for your help. The Empath's life purpose! To help and to heal! Yes, you go all in at the expense of yourself. The more you give as an Empath, the more the Narcissist takes and never replaces. Does this sound familiar?

I want you to understand that your energy is precious. You can't heal everyone, nor should you. Kathy once said something to me in a session, "Why do you think you have the right to impose your help on someone?" This came as I was telling her how someone I knew wouldn't be as reactive if they tried trauma therapy, and I had suggested this to them. Kathy reminded me that everyone has their

71

own journey, and we are not meant to heal everyone, nor should we. We must be selective with our energy in order to keep our bodies healthy and our minds happy. The moment we are out of balance, our Karma shifts and we need to take a step back and reassess.

Being an Empath, it is really easy to get down on yourself or think of your gift as a curse because it's hard feeling all the energies of the world, taking on all the negative, all the stress. But there are beautiful things to being an Empath. If you can control your energy and build boundaries, the healing you can do for yourself can be life-changing, and the relationships you build will be strong, beautiful, full of growth, evolution, and healing. You have a gift, a gift that Source believed you were strong enough for, and you are! Look how far you've already come, all the adversity you've already faced, and here you are, still standing. I've said it before and ill repeat it again, give yourself the same grace, admiration, praise, and patience you would anyone else who has come his far on their journey!

Chapter 6

October 1st, 2019, 11:10 pm

What happened to me? Where did my happy go? I feel like it left with *my dog*. My purpose and my reason.

Jazzy loves me, but *my boy* needed me. He needed me to hold him and cuddle him. *He* gave me purpose. *He* gave Jazzy purpose. Jazzy and I are both lost. She is so sad, I can see it in her eyes, I can hear it in her sighs; I notice her sulky behaviour. She misses her baby as much as I do. She doesn't even ask to play anymore. Maybe she feels like she's lost purpose too. All because N needed to try to control and hurt us. Because his goal is to hurt.

It shocks me that there are people like that out there in the world. People that are so cunning and selfish and mean-spirited that they can fool the most careful people. I was careful! I thought I was being smart. I thought I picked the right one this time. I thought I had learned from my past relationships and I thought that I had broken the cycle, and every time I fell back into the same situation, only worse in some way. I thought I had done things right. But I hadn't. And then I blame myself for allowing things to get so bad.

Should I blame myself?

Should I blame him?

Should I blame at all?

Blame is such a terrible word. I project the responsibility elsewhere.

What I DID do, was take action. I got into counseling and took action.

Tired and fed up.

Done with unhealthy patterns.

Determined. That's what I am now.

Determined to break this pattern.

Determined to not let this happen again.

Determined to love myself and respect myself enough to not let this happen again.

Never will I let a man yell at me for hours and hours on end.

Never will I tolerate abuse of any kind.

Never will I ignore my intuition again.

I was always right.

Every time I thought he was lying I was right.

Every time I thought he was cheating I was right.

I was always right.

I hated that I was always right.

But I was always right.

I should have listened to myself.

When he said that if I ever put my foot down, we'd have issues, I should have done it anyways. I should never have let the disrespect get so bad.

But I sacrificed so much for *my dog*, and he stole him from me in the end.

I will fight. I will fight for my boy.

I will fight for what is right.

I will fight to show I am strong and that I am a woman of principle and that he cannot win by being cruel.

Kindness and goodness will win.

Truth and honesty will win.

I will be the change that others need to hear about.

There cannot be an oppressor without the oppressed, and I will no longer be weak, I am not weak.

A weak person cannot put up with what I did for as long as I did. The reason I am still here is because I have been strong. I was strong for my kids *[my dogs]*, and I will continue to be. I was and will always be an advocate for them and for all women who fight and feel lost and defeated and deflated. For women who feel broken because a man projected his insecurities onto them.

[I want to be clear that abuse is not exclusively a woman's issue and Narcissism isn't exclusively a male trait. I realize how I generalized in this entry and I want to make those two points clear and take accountability for my generalizations]

Lessons:

- DON'T USE EMOTIONAL CRUTCHES: Emotional crutches are anything that helps you cope, or rather escape, the stressors or trauma. These are things or people. Typically, we turn to alcohol or drugs as emotional crutches, but then again, we can have people or pets or places as crutches; anything really. The issue is when that crutch is taken, or the expectations you put on those crutches aren't met, we do not have the emotional capability to cope differently. In my case, my emotional crutch was my dog. When N broke in and took him, I literally crumbled. Naturally, this was what N wanted. He wanted to find a way to hurt me, and he knew exactly how to do it. I put my happiness in something else, attached it to something impermanent rather than finding it within myself. This not only hindered my ability to cope but would always leave me unhappy and unfulfilled in my life. It kept me in a cycle where I looked for happiness in outside sources and it kept me, prevented me, from doing the real work on myself that I needed to find happiness, validation, and safety within.

It also left my emotions and identities fluid. Because I never had to look inwards for happiness, I never truly knew what made me happy. I never truly knew how to cope with emotions. My default was to shut down and hug *my dog*. Even after N took *my dog*, I got two kittens. Really, I fostered both kittens because Jazzy was so depressed and I wanted something to cheer her up, but then, once again, I attached our happiness to the kittens. I expected them and Jazzy to keep me happy and when I had hard days, I shut down with them. I needed to change my patterns. I needed to learn how to sit with my emotions but also process them and find happiness within myself. My kittens won't live forever, neither will Jazzy or Shaobear. Neither will Z, or my parents, or anything that I may attach my happiness to. If I continue with this pattern, with every heartbreak, I will break down more and more and continue to search for an outside source rather than do the work necessary to heal and grow and find everything I need within.

I feel like losing *my dog* was God's way of saying "You need to learn to cope on your own girl! You'll never learn to do that if you have *him* with you!" And I did. I remember going into my therapy session shortly after the incident, and I was a mess! I was even more of a mess than the day after the incident that led to N's his arrest. Even my counselor was shocked about how much of a wreck I was. That says a lot, doesn't it? When a trauma counsellor is shocked? But this forced me to grow and learn to cope on my own. To work through the trauma without relying on anything as a crutch. I learned that I needed to look inward, not outward, for emotional stability and growth. I learned that if I keep seeking validation and happiness without, I'll never learn to find it within.

So, I did. I dug deep, turned inwards, healed, or started to heal my inner child and found that the happiness I needed came from my confidence which came from finding and living my genuine and authentic self. Only then was I able to feel truly comfortable in my own skin, but that took owning my guilt, understanding my shame, my trauma, and finding my true purpose.

Without purpose in life, you will wander from project to project with no real sense of self or accomplishment. Finding your purpose requires you to identify your morals, your values, what you stand up for, and what you stand for. It takes confidence to know your true and authentic self and stand by that person regardless of the adversity. Finding a purpose doesn't just give you a goal to work towards, it forces you to get to know yourself on a much deeper level than you have ever explored before. Once you find that purpose, your tribe, and you really feel one with yourself, you won't ever attach your happiness to an outside source, and you'll never be in danger of losing that happiness. You won't care about what other people think or if they judge you. That's freeing!

It is important to note, that doing this may be one of the toughest things you in your lifetime. As I mentioned, speaking your truth, being your genuine and authentic self rarely makes you popular. Chances are, once you begin that journey, your circle will get smaller, and smaller. People will drop off, which is fine. In doing so, you will find the people that admire you for your strength, people that will align with your values and beliefs and will uplift you to be the most courageous and confidence self you ever have been.

Don't be afraid of the process because it's daunting and you worry about loss. Because with those losses comes immense gain!

- TAKE CHARGE OF YOUR LIFE AND WORK TOWARDS YOUR LIFE PURPOSE & ACT UPON IT: It is so crucial to find your purpose, your reason for being. Something we can throw ourselves into that also teaches us and helps us. Whatever ignites your passion, but also calms your soul. Something that provides you with healing and helping. I searched hard for something… what could I do. What was my purpose here? It literally took me 4 years to finally come back to finish this book – my purpose. Not because it took me so long to write it or edit it, but because I put myself and my passions aside for so long to help someone else with his. Again, this is the same thing I did with N; I clearly hadn't learned my lesson.

I put my novel aside and took jobs that I liked, but didn't pay, or paid but I hated. Just living day after day, trying to meet the expectations of society. Work the job, make the pay, pay the bills and debt, then work the job… repeat. I did do work I loved, but the pay was too low, and I wasn't able to get ahead let alone break even most of the time which left me unhappy and stressed. The jobs that did pay, I hated. Either customer service where you get yelled at regularly, or a company that caused me so much trauma I left due to Narcissistic abuse in the workplace. Both those latter jobs paid great, and had good benefits, but my health was suffering. At one point, I had multiple ulcers. I needed the benefits to pay for the medication I needed for the ulcers, but would I have the ulcers if I wasn't so stressed out? If I didn't have ulcers, I wouldn't need the benefits to pay for the medication to take care of the ulcers caused by the work that I do that I feel like I need because of the benefits I need for my medication that is caused by the work that I do.

When you put it that way, it sounds like lunacy, right? But this is the culture we are bred into, the mindset we are conditioned to follow from the day we are old enough to work to the day we pass. Very few of us get to do what we love every single day; so, if you do, feel blessed! But for all those struggling to find your place, your passion, your purpose, dig deep. Turn inwards and think, before the conditioning, before the worry and anxiety of the social norms and expectations, before the bills and the cost-of-living concerns, before the mindset of lack, what did you want to do? What was your passion?

I'm not saying drop everything and go (like I did) but find your purpose and start there! Start small, start anywhere but just start!

I found my purpose – to help and share my life and my experiences with others. I absolutely realize how fortunate I am; maybe – definitely not – financially, but I have been blessed with having the opportunity to go to trauma therapy, to turn inwards, to heal, to move forward and to find my true self and my true purpose: this book and wherever it takes me. Which in my perspective, makes me right beyond measure. I truly do believe everything happens for a reason and I believe we are meant to heal to help heal and this is how I can do that. Share my experiences and what I have learned along the way.

For a long time, I was told to heal in silence, to keep this journey to myself. People's opinions had me questioning myself. "What are people going to think about the book?", "What are people going think about you?", "Will people get mad at me about the content?" Then I realized, the kinds of people who are against this book will be for their own personal reasons, whether it's because they had a part in the negative experiences, whether it's because they enabled it or whether they see a part of themselves in it. Either way, none of those reasons have to do with me and furthermore, if they do read this book, I hope it helps them heal as well. This book is intended to heal and to help heal, and not putting it out would be an injustice. Not sharing what I learned would be gatekeeping of the highest. There are so many people out there who cannot attend counseling for many different reasons, and healing should not be a well-kept secret. Healing helps everyone and should be shared.

That is my purpose and my reason for pain. To heal and help heal.

- WE ALL HAVE A ROLE TO PLAY IN EVERY SITUATION: It is super easy to blame someone else for things that happened to you. Especially when it is a situation where you truly have been victimized. But the reality of it is, there is always a part we played, always a role we took and a way we enabled our own pain. This is going to be a difficult concept for many to accept, but understanding the role you played and how you enabled the situation is the first step to being able to protect yourself from getting into that situation again.

Every situation has 2 sides, an action and a reaction or an action and a response. A response will control the situation, but a reaction will only perpetuate it. In a situation where someone is experiencing Narcissistic abuse, it is very common to be reactive and reactive abuse is real and what a Narcissist thrives on. This is where they get to gaslight, deflect, project and blame your reactions to their behaviour, rather than how their behaviour caused your reactions.

We've all been in that situation at least once where someone triggers you so much that you react, and the focus is then your reaction rather than the action that caused it. The reaction perpetuates the issue. Keep in mind reactions don't need to be big shows of emotion. No reaction is also an action, also a reaction, truly. When you react like it is ok, the action doesn't bother you (because you want to avoid an issue), that is, in itself, a reaction to the Narcissist's action and enables their behaviour. It keeps the patterns and cycles alive.

Sort of a catch-22, isn't it? That is in essence, the entire relationship with a Narcissist is a double-edged sword; damned if you do and damned if you don't.

There is always something to learn from and to grow from; some lessons in there to take into the future. This requires realization followed by action. It was **easy** for me to blame my ex for the things that happened. **He abused me. He was arrested, and he was the problem. Right? Right!** But wait, I'm not absolved of blame here. Why did the abuse go on for so long? Because I allowed it; I set the bar for how I was going to be treated and didn't do anything to change it. Was I scared to? Yes. Did he threaten to leave if I "put my foot down"? Yes. Did I enable and accept my position? Yes. Did I have unhealed trauma that caused me to enable? Also, yes.

What I should have done was set the bar high and kept it high. I should have respected myself enough to put my self-respect over my distorted feelings. But what have we been talking about this entire time? About self-confidence? It takes time to turn inwards and heal in order to find you, be you, understand you and be able to do better. That takes self-reflection and the ability to self-reflect. I wasn't in the right place to know or do the healing I needed to yet. I had lessons I needed to be shown and to learn from.

This leads to my next point:

- DON'T WORRY OR TRY TO CONTROL THE TIMELINE: I remember in grade 7, my teacher asked us to write a letter to ourselves and not to open it until we were 21 (I think); I can't quite remember the age. Well, I found it and opened it when I was in my 20s and I was stunned at how ignorant the young me was! I had assumed that by the age of 29, I would be married with a house and kids, and I would be a figure skating coach and doing that as a living. Wow, right? At 29 I was nowhere near where my letter assumed I'd be. I had finally ended another toxic relationship (patterns) and I was working nights at a factory. I had started seeing a new but also toxic man from work and was finishing up the last bit of my first degree. I was living with my brother, renting a room. Does that tell me that I failed the mission? Absolutely not. It tells me that a grade 7 version of myself truly knew nothing about life except for the expectations that society puts on women and men. Must have a good job, must buy a house, must have a family before 30. Well, here I am at 38, still not there yet and I'm ok with that.

I bought a house, set up a nursery, separated, sold my part of the house, moved into a small apartment with my dog, quit my toxic job, and started back on my book. In the time before and after that, I realized I have bilateral PCOS, and conceiving is difficult. I realized that in my younger years, I was in no shape either financially or emotionally, to have and raise a child. I realize that I wouldn't have wanted children with any of the men I was with in the state in which I was with them, or I the state in which I was living! The old me, still living with trauma, still ignoring her inner child, still without healthy boundaries. Not someone emotionally ready to raise a human being.

I've had this discussion with my mom in the past; about whether or not it's responsible for me to have children. Admittedly, there are a lot of mental health afflictions in my family on both sides and the struggle has been felt from generation to generation. Depression and anxiety are high in my family and there were times when I felt I was danger to myself. Do I want to take the chance to pass that on to another when I, myself. have said it's unfair for anyone to live this life? No, because I feel that's a little unfair. On the other hand, do I feel like now, at this stage in my life, I'd be able to help mitigate that? Yes. I believe I would be a healthy parent. Big questions, big debate.

It's also worth noting that societal issues and influences no longer bother me. When people don't want kids, I don't find that odd. When people want a big family, I think that's amazing. To each their own. My perspective really changed when I realized that having children might not be in the cards for me. I realized that even if I don't have children, I am still whole as a woman and a person. Being a woman is not defined by motherhood, and motherhood shouldn't be a measurement as to how whole of a woman you are. It is equally as valid to choose you, yourself, your growth, and your career over having kids. Not having kids does not make you any less of a woman or any less of a human being. Alternatively, just because I may have complications having children, does not mean I cannot have children, or my own biological children. There are several ways a woman can have a biological, or non biological child in today's world and just because you haven't birthed your own children, doesn't make you any less of a mother.

It always struck me as awfully hypocritical when people ask women when they are having kids, but not usually men. Probably because we as women are expected to bear children. Society has structured us to believe that unless we act as the baby maker, our existence is not yet complete. But what about men? If men don't have children, are they viewed as less of a man? Less complete? No, because they do not carry the child within their bodies, which means the child isn't automatically seen as an extension of him, and therefore, necessary to be complete in his existence.

It's also shocking that in today's word, if, as women, we decide to pursue our career over motherhood, we are still (generally) viewed as selfish, self-serving, self-centered. If we go for higher profile positions and make the same decisions and act the same way as our male counterparts, we are viewed as aggressive or cut-throat. But for a man to do the same, he's viewed as the breadwinner, the head of the family and is praised for his hard work, drive, and determination. These social constructs impose harm on us and the way we view ourselves and our purpose in life.

Well, I've decided for myself that I will no longer live guided by those constructs. I will not be concerned with how old I am, if my have or haven't had children yet, or if my career, growth, and mental health take precedence. Putting myself first is the only way I can be the best for anyone around me and I am not apologetic about that.

Chapter 7

October 4, 2019, 2:16 pm

I saw a psychic today. Felt like I needed some guidance, some direction so my mom took me. My mom is very spiritual, and I think this was for her just as much as it was for me. Whatever affects me also affects her so getting some clarity really helps us both.

The Psychic told me some things I already knew and some things I feel like I needed to hear.

- ■ I need to do things with my hands and my mouth.

- ■ I need to be by water and to align my chakras.

- ■ I need to cleanse daily. Ill will follows me and this is why I need to cleanse.

- ■ I give too much but I do not receive from people.

- ■ I am kind but there are 3 people in my life who are close to me who are jealous of me, my life, my love life, and my family. They pretend to wish me well but do not truly wish me well.

- ■ I need to look with my eyes open, but my mouth shut because there is a lot of gossip.

- ■ I must be careful and aware of who I have in my circle.

- ■ I need to remove my ex-boyfriend – the man was bad from the start. I have a pattern of relationships – bad relationships.

- ■ 2020 is a year of new beginnings and ending negative ties: I will be shocked at who people are that wish me ill, but I must be able to move forward without them.

- ■ I need to focus to finish projects that I start. Aligning my chakras will help with this.

■ I need to meditate daily.

■ I need to move forward and listen to my heart and not my head; my head is clouded but my heart is pure.

■ Too many people are trying to force me in the direction they want me to go in, but I must listen to myself and my heart and go in the right direction. Do not allow others to cloud my judgment.

■ The stars will align for me in 2020.

■ Something is blocking my aura and I need to realign.

■ I will be comfortable, but I will always want more and feel like I am meant for more.

■ Not meant to be behind a desk for work.

Lessons:

- GROWTH WILL CHANGE YOUR MINDSET AND BRING YOU BACK TO YOUR HEART: I remember at the time of that reading, I was a little skeptical. I hadn't yet fully accepted the idea of energy, connecting with, and listening to spirit, and channelling messages. Now that I've been expanding and practicing my own abilities, previously blocked by trauma and fear, I realize just how accurate that psychic was.

- Working with my hands and my mouth? Yup – I make jewelry, I am writing a book. I love to kickbox and personal train. I also am working on my psychic abilities to hone them so I can deliver accurate messages to help heal. I also use my voice to stand up for what I believe in and hope through this book, I can continue to do that.

- Need to be by water? Yes, 100%. I have realized in the past few years that being by water, listening to water, washing dishes, watering the garden, and meditating in the shower is where I get my messages, and where I am able to calm my mind and my soul.

- I need to cleanse daily and I do. I cut chords every night, I cleanse often and rid myself of those negative energies.

- The three people in my life who were truly jealous showed themselves and weeded themselves out in 2020. Coincidence? No such thing. I have also learned to reel in my energy. To set boundaries to be able to protect my energy so I can use it more wisely and distribute it wisely.

- I had a pattern of bad relationships, awful relationships. Friendships too. For the longest time I was unable to rid myself of these individuals. But with healing and growth, they weeded themselves out and made room for others. Some people from the past that were also on a healing journey and found me again, and others that were new and wonderful and aligned with the person I was becoming.

- 2020 was definitely a change and I was very shocked at the people that cheered for me but weren't actually on my team. I also knew, I always had a feeling, but I wasn't in tune with my intuition, my energy, and my spirit team, and I didn't listen. I had a hard time letting go of control, of letting life unfold and follow the signs. I felt like needed to control the outcome and I let myself lead with anxiety rather than let the universe, Source, and my spirits lead me to what was right while removing what wasn't.

- I need to finish projects I start – case in point, this book. Started in 2019, finishing up in 2023. Although, as I said, everything happens for a reason. I genuinely forgot about that reading until I re-read the entry to reformat my lessons. This is indeed the 3rd time I am editing this book because the past 2 times I felt I was still leading with pain, and the last time I picked up this book was in 2020. It's been a while and now that I am finishing this book, I'm able to see how much I've grown, how much I've changed, and I can accept that the less healed version of myself wasn't ready for the blessings that are to come. I had a lot of healing to do, just like I still do. But the lessons I've learned since 2020 have put me in a position where I am truly ready to accept blessings and maintain them.

- I need to listen to my heart rather than my head because my head is clouded, and my heart is pure. Back in late 2019, early 2020 I'm sure this would have been taken very literally. Dealing with N, trying to get him out of my life, going through therapy, hitting rock bottom, of course my head was clouded. I truly felt at the time I couldn't trust my heart, so this message didn't have the right context to me. But now, 3 years later, re-reading that entry, I understand. I get it! My head was clouded, not by the recent trauma, but by the childhood trauma that taught me that red flags were normal and normal wasn't necessarily safe. A distorted view of normal, or roles, or expectations and coping mechanisms. This is what clouded my mind, blocked my intuition and my connection with my spirit guides and my higher self. But in my defense, at the time, listening with my heart was difficult; if it had been up to me, I would have made bad decisions. I remember specifically, while the police were looking for N to arrest him, I stayed at a friend's house for over a week in a different city for safety reasons, and I remember missing him. Why? Trauma bonds. Not because I did miss him, because, there was truly nothing to miss. But I was trauma bonded. Meanwhile, when I was 21 and dated Z, I ran away because the love he just freely gave me seemed without condition and my brain told me that was a red flag/danger! Only now do I realize that I needed to heal myself. Only then I could listen to my heart rather than my head. I could learn to lead with love rather than trauma. Lead with an empathetic heart rather than a mind overrun with trauma responses.

2020 was also the year I reconnected with Z and we bought a house in 2021. My life changed drastically and got everything I had been asking for, but I clearly wasn't ready for that kind of abundance. I proved it by falling back into old patterns. There was still so much to heal and learn. So here is to another chapter in my life, taking these lessons with me and letting the chips fall where they may.

- HEALING IS A PROCESS, NOT A DESTINATION: My therapist once referred to healing as an onion. As you peel back those healed layers from old triggers and traumas responses, you will find more that come up. Once you heal those triggers and responses, a new set will show up. This is why healing is a lifelong journey, not a destination. No one will wake up one day and realize, "I'm healed! Amazing, watch me go take on this world as a perfect human being!" We will always have an aspect of ourselves that we should work on, and if we believe we are perfect and do not ever require more healing, we are leading with Ego. If we see healing as a process to a final destination, or having an end goal, we will continuously be disappointed with our results, and we will miss the most important part of healing, the process! The process is where the important lessons are learned, the important self-reflection is done, and where we really find out who we are. If we focus on the end result only, we will never be able to truly immerse ourselves in the process where all the magic happens. That's like wanting to be fit but never wanting to live a healthier lifestyle and then getting frustrated when nothing changes.

Here are some important points to healing and the process:

a. Healing is a process, and you will hit significant milestones with still more work to do and healing doesn't just happen if you only do it for an hour in therapy. You have to practice all day, ever day! You are continuously working on using those coping mechanisms to control anxiety or depression or worry or concern. No one can tell you when you have "finished" healing a stage in your life, or if 2 years is the standard to be "healed enough". Healing is a process, and everyone progresses at different rates. Don't compare your journey to someone else's and don't rush the process.

b. Healing looks different to everyone. I remember when I was starting my healing process, I had my own way of healing. Similar to most, I thought. I started following certain pages, started following positive and motivational pages, workout pages, and higher vibrational pages. Influential people, motivational people, people who shared in my experiences and who have healed from their traumas and are sharing their stories to inspire and motivate others. I started unfollowing some people for different reasons as well. I started cleaning up what I ingested and surrounded myself with; what people, media, books, and environment. I also stopped following people who practiced toxic positivity. It is very common to fall into the "good vibes only" phase and stay there when you are healing, but this, in itself, is unhealthy. Healing isn't about always being happy and positive; it's about understanding that we have a full range of emotions, and we need to learn how to process each of them in a healthy manner. If we only allow "good vibes", we are masking, we are enabling, and refusing the hard parts of growth that are necessary for emotional development. We must also learn how to live our authentic self. This means evaluating what you value. Maybe you value equity and equality and that means standing up to oppressors. This comes with having difficult discussions on controversial topics and learning to manage the emotions that come as a result. This is all growth and all necessary for your evolution.

      c. I started changing how I talked to myself and about myself and tried to actively control my thoughts because that is what you manifest and create and what then attracts the environment around you. I also started sharing my story slowly. I found this therapeutic. Speaking of what I have kept such a secret, been buried under, and full of shame. You cannot heal an issue, if you refuse to admit there is one in the first place. There were others who didn't like what I was sharing. Some people tried to convince me that I needed to delete social media altogether to heal. Some people thought I should consider going away to heal. Everyone had a version of healing that was their own and couldn't understand my healing methods and process. And that is ok. Just like we all learn differently and feel differently, then we must also heal differently. And though we may not understand another's ways of healing, we should respect it and support the individual through it. I'm very thankful that I did not delete social media or jump on a plane and run from my problems; because essentially, that is what I would be doing, running, and avoiding. I needed to sit in my feelings, dissect them, understand the root cause of them and take control to heal, not distract myself, run away from my issues or turn to toxic positivity.

I reconnected with some people who have made a huge difference in my life and shared the same mindset, and some that don't, but each of them have the same underlying values and kindness, empathy and understanding for humanity and the complexities of life and healing. Changing my surroundings, realizing which people/energies should be allowed have access to mine and which shouldn't and pulling myself back from my head to my heart made such a huge difference. It's incredible the kind of energy you pull in (as an empath or not) from the people you surround yourself with. If you surround yourself with negative people with a constant victim mentality who believe they are above healing, you aren't going to be in a mindset that is conducive to healing. But if you are around people that understand, that are supportive of your journey and however you take it (as long as you are not hurting yourself or anyone else), then your mindset changes, your energy changes, you feel lighter and are able to then speak more kindly to yourself as you aren't filling your energy with toxicity that you then turn back onto yourself.

d. You get what you put in. You can't expect to make leaps and bounds in your healing journey if you only do the work once a week in session. You must work at healing; you will progress if you invest in the process. Healing is a process and takes training and practice. You need to spend time investing into that process. You need to work at it and do the hard things. It hurts to dig deep and being in your own head is scary. But it must be done. When I was healing, I read on narcissism, narcissistic abuse, on emotional blackmail all the way to the court system. I read about all that to understand my past and the perpetrator. Who was I? Who was he? What have I become and how? His influence? Society's influence? Family influence?

I needed to recognize the patterns, recognize the trauma, understand how that contributed to all those emotionally abusive relationships and recognize all those red flags I kept ignoring and why I kept ignoring them. I faced the hard issues and dealt with them. This is the only way to ensure you stop those patterns and habits and form new habits, new patterns, and utilize the right coping mechanisms to triggers in future situations.

If someone said to you, "this journey is going to be really hard, really taxing, and you have to work on it every single day, but in the end, you will have emotional fulfillment! Or you can continue the way you are going, experiencing the same painful cycles over and over again", which would you choose? To go through the dirt for a lifetime of fulfillment? Finding self-confidence and living your authentic and true self, or would you prolong your suffering, masking, people pleasing, rat racing, and spinning that hamster wheel for the rest of your life because healing is hard?

You can't take shortcuts with healing either. And you can't fake it. You must go all in and put in the work. And understand that, in order to heal, you must commit. You must commit to the process, the methods, and to yourself every single day with every single decision. You deserve your own commitment more than anyone else!

e. Lastly, you are worthy of love whether or not you love yourself. I hate that saying, "How can you expect someone to love you if you don't love yourself?". That is incorrect my friends! Just because you are struggling with your self worth, doesn't mean that others don't see it within you. Just because you struggle with self love, doesn't mean that others aren't capable of loving you!

Will it be difficult to accept love if you don't love yourself? Yes. Of course. Without self love, you lack self confidence and will take everything (even the most well-meaning comments or advice) with a tinge of insecurity, and everything will seem like a personal attack because of how you feel about yourself. But that doesn't mean you aren't worthy of love. Love heals, and if you keep avoiding it, or believe you don't deserve it, this will prolong your suffering. If someone loves you, knows you to the root and still loves you, it's because they see something in you that you do not yet see in yourself. But heal, and you will. Accept that love, because it heals and moves mountains! You are worthy of it, I promise you!

Chapter 8

October 6, 10:30 ish

Got a new book to read, "Girl Wash Your Face" and I just finished reading a chapter about helping keep promises and commitments to yourself. If you can't keep a promise to yourself, do you really value yourself? This behaviour and pattern mold your mental training is the premise of the chapter. This molds your actions and therefore yourself.

This was deep.

This got me thinking.

I am SO guilty of this procrastinating and telling myself:

- I'll do it later

or

- I meant to do it today but I'll do it tomorrow.

I'm more apt to keep a commitment to a friend; to someone else, than I am to myself.

Why?

I started pondering why. I started to think, "If I can't even commit to keeping my word to myself, do I really respect myself? How much do I really value myself if I don't care enough for myself? And if that's the case, then how good of a friend am I to others?

How often do I flake on myself, and how often do I flake on others? That's not fair to others or myself. If I'm not committed to myself, and investing in myself and giving my all to those investments, how can I improve? If an athlete wants to be a well-rounded athlete, they must put 100% in all areas: the gym, their diet, practice… if I truly want to be better, I have to keep those promises to myself to do things that make me better.

I started to think of all the things I put off,

- How long have I meant to bring those bags of clothing to goodwill?

- How many times have I said I would clean the fish tank, and just stared at it?

- How many days have I missed going to the gym? Or stopped for months all together?

- How many times have I promised to make up Jazzy's missed afternoon walk?

- How many times have I told myself that I would write in my journal or publish a book or start blogging again?

Far too many times. I need to respect myself more and stop being a "yes" person. Like the book says, be careful with your "Yesses". Be sure you can commit to that "yes" and make sure you follow through with that "yes". Including to myself.

I need to respect myself enough to truly keep commitments to myself and becoming a better friend to others. A better version of myself for others.

I need to be better and want to be better. That means getting out of my own head and retraining myself to calm my anxiety and pushing through each time I want to say "later" or "tomorrow" to really and truly be a woman of my word.

I need to lead by example.

Lessons:

- WE TRULY DON'T KNOW OURSELVES UNTIL WE ANALYZE OURSELVES: Wow, this entry brings me back and made me want to puke a little when I read one of my originally written lessons. It was all about creating habits, sticking to them, making that commitment to yourself, and respecting yourself enough to stick to them. Then I realized, wait, there is a reason that I (and others) procrastinate, and it has nothing to do with not respecting myself.

I recently went down a few months of Tik Tok rabbit holes and realized that I may have ADHD which would explain all those issues! I do have c-PTSD which can also presents as ADHD, so the verdict is still out. Either way, the overwhelm, the procrastination, the pseudo-doom piles and the consistent forgetfulness can be crippling and discouraging. I'm telling you; I have had a bag of mail from the old owners of my home that I had meant to "Return to sender". Usually, I could leave it in my mailbox, but over Covid, the mail delivery people stopped taking those back, so I needed to drive them over to the post office. Well, in true fashion, I put the mail in a plastic bag on the kitchen counter next to the front door to be able to remind myself to take the mail to the post office. Over a year later, I sold my part of the house, and the mail is still sitting there, on the hook, next to the front door in the house and hasn't been returned. Which reminds me to go grab it next time I go over there so I can FINALLY bring it to the post office.

Now, this has absolutely nothing to do with me not respecting myself or not having a routine and has everything to do with damage from trauma and possibly being neurodivergent. But if we compare ourselves to people who aren't, if I consistently compare myself to my best friend who isn't living with trauma or and is neurotypical, I will always feel insecure and like I don't respect myself when in fact, I truly do.

Truth be told, the world isn't made to accommodate people who don't learn the same way, or act the same way, or process the same way as the socially constructed status quo. All my life I was made to feel inadequate or like I didn't try hard enough compared to others. Even in school, my teachers always sent home notes or report card comments that I don't apply myself, that I don't pay attention, that I am easily distracted. All these times I thought I was a bad student, or not as smart as all the other kids because my grades were just average. My brother on the other hand would make honour roll without even trying. But as the saying goes, "Everybody is a genius. But if you judge a fish by its ability to climb a tree, it will live its whole life believing that it is stupid".

When I made it to university, which I never imagined I'd be accepted to, I realized how I needed to learn to retain information, why I was freezing up and forgetting things during tests and what was the most effective way for me to retain information and stay calm during exams. I learned the ways I needed to learn and was able to manage my own expectations, rather than be subjected to the expectations of someone that compared me to someone "normal" and held that as the bar to meet.

We have been taught from such a young age whose opinions we should value and what we need to conform to, by the people we trust the most. We then grow up in a world where the people of authority, the people we are told to listen to, like parents or Teachers, don't understand or have the time or resources to help people who don't fit that neurotypical mold. We believe their opinions matter most, and when they get frustrated because we don't fit, we internalize and believe we are wrong. We then grow up believing we are backwards or less than, rather than understanding the world is filled with people who don't fit the mold. We were simply never allowed the opportunity to shine because society has tried to fit us into a mold that kept us restricted and wasn't made for us. Our ego then keeps us from who we truly are because we have been conditioned to believe we are wrong, different, not smart. I say it all the time, 2+2 is 4, but so is 3+1.

The important thing is to know yourself, have some grace with yourself and be open to being different. There is nothing to say that being neurodivergent is bad; it's just a different way of being.

Be open to learning about yourself and don't let your ego get in the way of accepting different ways of being. The Ego is the most destructive thing to our healing journey. A little ego is required for survival and protection, but too much ego will leave you closed to possibilities that are meant to bring health and happiness.

- BE PATIENT WITH YOURSELF: I stated this earlier, but it is crucial to enjoy the process and the journey. Most people, during their healing process, only focus on the end goal, the healed version of themselves but miss all the small lessons along the way because they are hyper-focused on the outcome only. If you don't stop, pause, be present and let the process unfold as it should, you will miss all the small lessons that present themselves, and all those small steppingstones are necessary to get you to the next stage. You can't get to the top floor of a walk-up if you don't use the stairs. The top floor will never come down to meet you where you are. You need to make the climb.

The climb takes digging deep into the darkness. Feeling that darkness, sitting with it and sifting through it. Avoiding it means avoiding a massive part of the healing process. You cannot heal the darkness if you don't first address it, and if you never address it, this darkness, this hurt, this trauma will follow you around until you do. Lessons will present themselves repeatedly in different forms until we take a moment to recognize them and learn from them. For this, we must accept, explore, and sit with all our darkness, all our dark emotions. Each dark emotion has a great lesson to teach us. According to Sheri Van Dijk, MSW, RSW, a psychotherapist in Sharon, Ontario, Canada, emotions not only teach us but protect us. Anger is a cluster of emotions such as sadness, insecurity, and fear, and when we acknowledge these emotions, we can pinpoint what is triggering us and manage that emotion in a more productive manner. Frustration, for instance can mean we are internalizing. Fear is a great motivator to navigate risky situations and keeps us alert. Envy may drive us to pursuit of greater goals and experiences. Sadness can teach us about loss and grief. All of these emotions are important to be felt. If you choose not to feel them, you are then masking which is an unhealthy coping mechanism and isn't conducive to proper healing and management of your feelings and self.

- THE "Good Vibes Only" LIFESTYLE IS TOXIC: This mindset of "good vibes only", "I will only surround myself with positive people", "don't have time for your negative mindset", is TOXIC. It is not conducive to healing and does not actually raise your vibrations/energy. This mindset leaves you unbalanced. The pain doesn't go away just because you ignore it. Rather, it will come out in many other toxic ways as if masking isn't toxic enough.

Believing that you will raise your vibrations simply by accepting only positivity is performative and will leave you in the same stage of healing you started in. To truly, raise your vibrations, you need to heal every aspect of yourself. You need to dig deep into that darkness where your trauma is rooted. Only then, when you start at the root, will you actually grow, heal and evolve. Only then will you ascend to a new energetic level, a higher version of yourself which will then align you with people at that same energetic level.

I remember once, a friend told me that she didn't want to hang out with me because I was always "broke". And then, a few years later, when we reconnected, we hung out all the time until the situation with N happened. Then she told me that, given the situation, it was too much as she was living a "good vibes only" lifestyle. Only when I was on the up and up did she want to hang out. When I was down and out, she wasn't available. She only wanted to hang around people who were positive, who had no issues, who were able to fit her "good vibes only" lifestyle. She didn't want to address or talk about the hard things. Avoiding any message, or topic that was uncomfortable.

Yes, I had negativity I had to sift through, I had people I needed to weed out of my life, I needed to find myself and heal myself and to do that, I dug deep, to the darkest places that I never wanted to revisit, and I healed those layers, and levels. Naturally, almost effortlessly, people started to fall out of my life and others started to fall in. I was living my authentic self, and that's when Source will weed out the people you are no longer aligned with.

Once you have learned your lessons, healed whatever layer of trauma you needed to address and truly raised your vibrations, will Source, the universe, your Angels, whatever you choose to believe in, line up the opportunities for you! There is a catch though, as always. The moment you stop doing the work, the moment you become complacent in your life, it will all be snatched back. Another lesson telling you that you need to work to maintain what you have. A gift is a gift because you earned it, don't regress and lose it again. Keep working on yourself, keep focussing on yourself, reflect every single day on what situations you entered, how did you handle it, did you lead with love and an empathetic heart? Did you respond or react? Is there anything you learned? Is there anything you could have don't differently? Is this work? Yes. This is the homework the universe/Source wants you to complete to ensure you remain in your current energetic level. Recognize your blessings, stay present, keep learning, and keep growing so you can receive more of the abundance that is in store for you!

Chapter 9

October 9, 2019, 9:55 pm

It hit me as I was reading a chapter of "Girl Wash Your Face". I realized the person I was vs. the person I became while dating N. I always knew it, and I had admitted it, but I didn't always truly accept it myself. It started the very first time we talked about dating. Up to that point, me standing in his hallway, trying to have a serious conversation with him, he didn't even care enough about the conversation to stop washing the dishes. Something he barely ever did when we were together. After months of talking, watching "our" shows, *[mimicking a relationship]*, he tells me he didn't want a relationship. Did I walk away after that? No, I threw my self respect out the window and continued to hope. Why? Beats me. Maybe because he was good at pretending? He was great at talking and pseudo-apologizing, and every time he would call, I would go back running. Either way, that defining moment set the tone for our entire relationship. I put myself last, threw my self-respect away, and allowed the emotional abuse and manipulation. And when he was finally ready, stupid me, I jumped for joy like "FINALLY!"

Then he cheated 4 months in. I found the pics. I found the messages. I found the proof. He even called me that night, dead quiet in the background on a guy's night. We already had *our dog*. I was already moving in with him. I had given up my apartment, I was going back to school and not working since he asked me not to. What was I to do? So, I stayed. I allowed it. I condoned it by accepting his apology and by pretending to not know he was doing that almost every weekend.

The first night *[when we had our first fight]* he spent *[the entire night]* yelling at me for being upset with him, I allowed it. Each time he would stand over me yelling, *[I'd be]* sitting on the bed with the dogs, crying, apologizing to him for getting upset with him over something he did, in which I was perfectly reasonable and justified; I was allowing his behaviour.

When he punched the wall or broke my phone or shattered glass, I was allowing that behaviour and indirectly saying that was acceptable behaviour. I look back at that person and I wonder who the hell she was. How did I become her? Someone so far removed from the woman I once was. I talked about it with my trauma counselor; why I so desperately clung to him and his love. I know it sounds so cliché, but I have parent issues.

My parents did the best they could. My father was raised by a hard man. My grandmother was always working or taking care of the family. My father was the only surviving boy: 7 children of 14 survived and only one boy. He grew up *[being]* bullied. He doesn't show *[much]* affection *[in the way I needed it to be shown]*. I think this year was the first time he ever told me he loved me. He is a hard man raised by a hard man and grew up in a generation where discipline was physical and appropriate.

My mother grew up the total opposite. Her mother passed when she was 7. She is the youngest of 9 and was raised by her brothers and sisters and mostly taken care of by her father and then my dad. She learned how to parents as she went. She raised us while battling her own demons, in a new country with little support *[in a city where she didn't speak the dominant language]*. My brother always seemed to be the favourite. My parents always told me that they love us equally, but their actions spoke volumes. I spent a lot of my childhood seeking validation, love, and approval from my parents. I have been searching for the same thing in relationships; going for men who mirrored my father, emotionally unavailable. When they accepted me and loved me, I finally felt like I won their love and validation; something I feel I struggle to get from my father. This is what love looked like to me; difficult, and unspoken. Fighting for it and hoping for validation. Dating became the same; trying to satisfy my inner child, the one that never got what she needed. Never knew that love was about feeling safe, accepted, and respected. Not something you have to always fight for, earn, or show you're worthy of.

This realization did not come to me in an epiphany; it took a lot of therapy to calm that inner child and realize that no one but me could help her. No one but me can heal and protect her. No one but me can help her move past the backwards ideas of what she thinks she needs and discover what she truly requires to heal, and truly feel protected and safe.

This realization is what helped me find myself. Not find myself again, because before this I actually had no idea who I was. I thought I did, but I clearly had trauma I needed to properly work through. I thought I knew who I was, but clearly, I didn't because I kept falling back into the same patterns when it came to friendships and relationships. Now that I understand what I was missing, what I was trying to fill, what I was compensating for and what I was chasing and why, I can finally learn to grow and become the woman I need to be, to be the best version of me that I can be. I don't have all the answers, and I'm not sure what the end result will be. Maybe there will never be an "end result" because I will be constantly learning and growing through life; but I know what I was doing wrong, and what I need to do right. I know who I was, who I had become and who I want to be. I know that I have to respect myself and not allow my old needs to compromise my actual needs and wants and I know what standards I want to hold myself, and others to, and this I will not compromise.

Lessons:

- WE ARE THE GENERATION TO BREAK GENERATIONAL TRAUMAS: Yes, we are! This is our time to shine! I have a wonderful relationship with my parents now, and that is all thanks to therapy! Recovery is not just about learning about the Narcissist and it's not just about setting boundaries. If was that simple, well, we wouldn't be here, would we? It is our responsibility in a world where we have the resources, the information, and the knowledge, to identify and break those generational traumas and end the cycle. From a generation that doesn't believe in feeling, to a generation that understands feeling everything is the true key to growth. As the times change and evolve, as we know more and how to do better, we must commit to actually doing and being better. To reflect every time we react and understand where that reaction is coming from and how and who we want to be moving forward.

My parents are wonderful human beings and mean well. They did the best they could with the tools they had, but they both came from not only a different generation but they also had cultural traumas and norms that are outdated. Therapy really helped me put myself aside, center them and their traumas and understand that I have the opportunity to do better by them and for them. I have the tools to understand adapt, empathize and do better for those I love and the generation after me. And hopefully, doing my own work may even heal the generations before me.

Recovering from Narcissistic abuse is not just about learning to manage how you come out of the relationship but also understanding and correcting the elements of yourself that lead to these individuals having access to your life. Narcissistic abuse is total abuse and all encompassing, and your healing journey must be the same.

- HEALING MEANS GOING FORWARD, NOT BACK TO THE PERSON YOU WERE: Over my journey, I have spoken with people who were also healing, and I've heard so often, "I just want to be the person I used to be." My darlings, this is not growing, nor is this healing. This is reverting to the unhealed version of yourself. After reading that entry, I do NOT want to be that person again. That is the person that got me into this mess. The one that couldn't see red flags, the one that believed aggression against things is only against things (we later found out it WILL translate to aggression against people). That was the version of myself that believed you needed to prove you were lovable in order to be loved, and you weren't just loved for who you were, you were loved for how valuable an asset you were. That version of myself was raised by good people who had a lifetime of unhealed trauma. That version of myself makes me cringe. Reading through that post brought me right back to the actual incidents. I can actually visualize those times with vivid accuracy, yet anything before or after the incident is a blur. Again, my brain's way of protecting me from trauma that was too much to process at the time.

One incident was actually when I was sitting on my bed, apologizing to him after one of his rages. He threw a violent rage regarding how I became friends with one of my closest friends. We had both been involved with a narcissistic individual and bonded over the shared experiences. It was before N and I started dating and was truly not his business nor was it ever relevant or impactful to anything in our relationship. When I say rage, that's an understatement.

That night, I had a full-blown panic attack, and the next day, one of my professors pulled me out of seminar and told me I should go see a counselor because I was visibly distraught and unwell. My professor called ahead to advise the office of my arrival in case I didn't make it. I went to the school's counseling office, spoke with a trauma therapist who then called an ambulance to take me to the mental health ward. They gave me the option to go willingly, or the police would make me. I remember wanting to go, no resistance, just take me please. I don't remember the ride there, or much else before of after that conversation.

Once at the hospital, they asked if they could call anyone, and I said my parents but asked them not to tell N because I didn't want him to get mad. First, I understand how ridiculous that thought is. Why did I think he'd get mad? Because it would be an inconvenience to him, me being in the hospital. I cringe thinking that I was still afraid to upset him.

I believed my being in the hospital would trigger him because any slight inconvenience was a major issue. I was afraid he would get mad, project, and then rage again. Well, my parents called him, and he came rushing to the hospital. My parents then took us all out for lunch after I was discharged, and N and I went home. As soon as we got home, his demeanor changed. He was mad, angry, and felt inconvenienced just as I had imagined he would. He was angry with me because he had to leave work. He was angry with me because he had to rush from work to the hospital and blamed me for the fact that he drove over the speed limit. He said if he had gotten a ticket, it would have been my fault.

I internalized the entire situation. I believed I shouldn't have been honest, I should have approached the situation differently, I shouldn't have even told him how my friend and I met, but he asked. I should have lied. I even felt bad for being friends with her. She still is, to this day, one of the most amazing people I know. She truly is a blessing and I'm very thankful for her. N made me feel like it was wrong, toxic, when in fact, he was. And being the unhealed version of myself, I almost fell for it. That is the unhealed version of myself that I will never return to. This is the deterrent that keeps me on the right track.

WHO WAS I?! Unhealed from years of conditioning, generational trauma, and triggers that were deeply ingrained, and I was unable to heal because of people pleasing. Because I never examined my self worth, I never thought about how I felt about myself or my incredible lack of self esteem, but rather tied my self worth to how toxic people felt about me. So that begs the question, why on earth would I ever want to be her again? Why on earth would I heal to revert back to being a toxic person? The kind of person that got me into that messed up, terrifying, dangerous situation. That version of me is long gone and I've since levelled up and refuse to go back.

Healing is done by understanding and addressing your traumas, and being better than you were. If you are on this healing journey, reflect back, yes, but don't ever try to be that old, unhealed person again. Be better as you know better! Heal to help heal!

- THE NARCISSIST ALWAYS HAS A PLAN OF ATTACK AND A CHOSEN VICTIM: I don't believe people truly understand how awful, insidious, and long-lasting narcissistic abuse is. We are very inclined nowadays to say, THAT person's a Narcissist, and THAT person's a Narcissist; it has become a "buzzword" and that is very harmful to people who have truly endured abuse at the hands of an actual Narcissist. It minimizes our experiences and our trauma. We've gone over what defines a Narcissist, but it is important to remind you that narcissistic abuse starts even before the relationship begins and Narcissistic abuse is total abuse. The abuse is not specific to one element of your life, but all elements of your life. The goal of the Narcissist is not just control of a specific area, but to break you down until you are shell of yourself and deplete you completely in all ways. It's total control.

How did you end up with a Narcissist? It was planned. Orchestrated. You didn't randomly fall into an abusive relationship with a Narcissist. Do not blame yourself. If there is anything I want you to take away from this, it is that it is not your fault, but it is your responsibility to heal so that you don't end up in the same situation. There is a reason that you went through what you went through, and it's not because you deserved it or you caused it, or that you are the problem. Yes, you have traits, unhealed trauma as we have discussed that lead to you fall victim to these individuals, but they chose you; you were prey.

We are very inclined to internalize and blame ourselves when we are in or get out of an abusive relationship; "I'm so dumb. There were so many red flags. Why didn't I see them? How could I be so stupid?"

Stop right there.

First, let's assess the language we are using there. We already talked about being kinder to ourselves, changing the way we talk to ourselves, and having more grace and patience with ourselves.

Next let's address how Narcissists prey on their victims. They sought you out, did an assessment, and chose you for when they were ready. They probably saw that you were really kind, really caring, willing to do anything for people, had this shine about you, and had limited boundaries. You probably started out as a "situationship" that was at their convenience and due to your own trauma and anxious attachment style, need for validation and distorted view of love, you hoped they'd see how great you were, and win their affection. So, you kept trying to prove yourself. You went above and beyond and extended every kindness. All this time, they were playing their game, pushing your boundaries, and seeing how much they can get away with. They'd plant little seeds in conversation, and being the open book that you are, you probably unintentionally told them about all your traumas, loves, and passions and that was exactly the information they needed to rope you in. They used your trauma to try to relate by pretending to share in experiences. They played the victim which appealed to your empathetic and nurturing nature. They mirrored your values and beliefs, your likes and dislikes.

N was great at this. I always thought he was a great listener. Quiet, but always knew exactly what to say. We had all the same interests: animals, camping, and valued family. Turns out he never camped, he never wanted to see his family, and although he acted like he loved my dog at the beginning, after we got a dog together, he started telling me how much he hated labs (Jazzy is a black lab mix). He never failed to slip that in whenever he could. I don't know how many times I begged him to go on vacation or camping. Camping was a hard no, and the one time we planned a vacation that he agreed to, he caused a fight about it just before the trip (which was my best friend's wedding), because he didn't want to waste money or time on a trip to see someone he didn't know get married (worth noting that I was paying for the trip). Clearly resentful of someone's happiness; a staple Narcissistic trait. The situation wasn't about him, it was about someone else, therefore, he felt inconvenienced. It's also super important to understand that any event where there is a show of emotion, a Narcissist will feel uncomfortable and try to sabotage, because they are fundamentally unable to relate and therefore get triggered. They also need to control something, anything and everything. In this case, the trip wasn't his idea and therefore he felt a loss of control which he needed to regain. I ended up canceling the trip, and we broke up not long after.

My point? You were not random, you were chosen. Not only do narcissists use everything you share with them against you, but they have a plan, orchestrated and executed at the right time. Again, it is not your fault that you got into this situation. You have traumas that you didn't know you had to work on, toxic behaviours that you needed to heal. It is, however, your responsibility to heal to do better next time.

Chapter 10

October 19th, 2019, 10:15 am

35 and it's scary. Yesterday I was thinking, "I'm 35, and what do I have to show for it?".

- I work in a call center and hate my job.

- I have an Honours degree I can't finish because of my current financial situation.

- I'm broke.

- Going through trial with my ex-boyfriend.

- I feel stuck.

- All I have is a car that isn't yet paid off.

Then I opened my book, and I was at a chapter on this exact thing, as if it was a sign.

- Don't compare your journey to others.

- God has a plan and everything will unfold in the right time.

- Everything, good and bad, happens for a reason.

Sometimes this is hard to believe, but I do believe it nonetheless. It sucks when you feel stuck, or behind in life. You see everyone else living a life they love and gaining success, and you are still where you were when you were in your 20s, only thing different now is, you are nearing your 40s. Somehow, I thought I would be farther along in life.

- A career, not just a job.

- Maybe another book published.

- Financially stable.

- Having travelled more.

- A house to my name, if even a tiny home.

It can be discouraging. But then I pull myself back to the idea that everything does happen in its own time.

- I got out of a terrible relationship.

- I entered counselling.

- I am healing from many traumas as a result.

- I will be healthier for myself and for others as a result.

THIS IS BIG!

This is ending patterns I would not have been able to end otherwise. Patterns I would not have recognized otherwise. And that in itself is much farther along than many people.

And that is a win.

And that is the foundation I need to be truly successful and genuinely happy in life and with my life.

Lessons:

- ALLOW YOURSELF THAT DOWN TIME: Reading that entry made me realize just how much my mind races and how hard it is to shut it off! Truly, healing can be such a trip. One minute your mind is racing with ideas and answers and the next you are laid out on the couch for days. But this doesn't make you lazy. This means you are healing. Healing is exhausting, truly. Traumas and triggers resurface that need to be healed, you are more sensitive to people's energy, you have sleep disturbances, going from no appetite to not being able to satiate cravings, women have menstrual cycle changes, feeling lonely, lost and detached. Being in such a high state all the time creates an irregulated central nervous system and hypervigilance. Always being in fight or flight or freeze or fawn, contributes to stress and increased cortisol and all that takes a toll on your body. Feeling emotions you have previously suppressed, having to process them, finding your triggers and trauma responses, and learning to manage those; all that is very tiring and takes a lot out of you mentally and physically. We also forget to take into consideration that your brain and body is actually physically healing from real damage and how much energy this requires. Sleeping more, lack of energy, lethargy, brain fog, flu like symptoms are all normal and by no means an exhaustive list of effects. Everyone wants the glow-up, but no one talks about the journey through it and the toll it takes on the body.

Not only is the mental and physical aspect of regulating and healing exhausting, but there is the spiritual aspect as well. You are changing your vibration. Your energy is shifting. Your body is adjusting. Your mind and soul are evolving and healing and just like growing pains, this uses up much of your energy! When you are going through a spiritual awakening, you may feel dull, lethargic, tired or cold. You may have headaches and body aches as well. These are all real symptoms. It takes a lot of work for your body to adjust to the new energy you are stepping into, so give yourself some grace and be kind to yourself and let yourself evolve and allow yourself to rest.

Society has taught us that if we are not moving, we are not being productive. If we rest, we are lazy. Life and the body aren't made to be on the go all the time. Rest is needed, and I don't mean just the barely 8 hours you may get a night. I mean rest, relaxation, meditation, feeding your soul, and recharging. This is especially crucial to Empaths. We take on so much and give so much and eventually run dry. We burnout and we didn't even mean to. All this to say, don't be so hard on yourself when you feel this way. When you feel like you'd rather nap, read, or take a bath or a walk. Don't feel bad when you don't respond to that email or text message. Don't feel bad if you'd rather spend time with yourself than with other people. I know you have a guilty conscience that comes with being such a beautiful soul, but set that aside and understand that self-love and self-care are necessary. Sometimes doing nothing is more productive than trying to do it all.

I used to get down on myself for not following the schedule I had planned in my head. I wanted to be more productive! Be the best me possible! Use my energy wisely! But what is wiser than using your energy to heal and rest and recharge? That is the best way to use your energy! Just like when you go to the gym and do a huge leg day; do you feel bad for not doing more legs the next day because you're sore and healing? No, you change muscle groups to give your legs a break, some rest, and some time to heal. The same goes for your mind and soul. It is crucial to take that downtime for recovery.

- IT'S THE SMALL WINS THAT MAKE THE BIGGEST DIFFERENCE: The destination is not reachable without all those little steppingstones in between. When I was healing, I was focused on the little things, not the goal. Of course, I looked toward the goal (at the time, it was just to stop feeling the way I did and to stop falling for the same toxic people), but I didn't realize that the goal would change and evolve so many times with each evolution.

With each step, I learned something new about myself and my goals changed. As I discovered more about myself and realized how much I had to offer, and the goals kept evolving and getting bigger. I realized I had been playing small forever, and that served no one, especially not me. With every stage of healing, with every layer of that onion peeling open, I discovered things about myself that altered my interest, grew my values, and added to my ethics. Each goal became bigger, seemingly unattainable, yet I smashed it. Nothing was impossible. I kept going, kept growing. Even through those awful tower moments, I was able to see the lesson in the event rather than sit and wallow in resentment. That, in and of itself, is a win. That is success.

I learned how to handle situations. I learned how to manage some triggers, and I learned how to respond vs. react to certain situations. I became a big fish in a little pond and wanted more. Is it scary going to a bigger pond? Yes, but that means so much more opportunity to grow! So many more amazing people to meet and learn from. So many more lessons to learn to become the most authentic, genuine, and strong version of yourself. By the time you know it, you've hit goal after goal without even realizing it because you have been so immersed in the moment, the lessons, and the experiences. That is growth; learning how to be present and enjoy and learn rather than live with so much anxiety from trying to control the outcome, or even being afraid of the outcome.

It's really easy to miss those small wins. They come and go by so quickly. Being present, taking a moment in solitude to reflect or journaling is so helpful to keep track of your amazing progress. It's also important to take a moment and look back at journal entries from a different perspective to realize and assess how much you've grown and celebrate that! Celebrate you! Even going back and reading these journal entries and the lessons I wrote back in 2020, I see how much I have grown. I was just telling Z the other day that I reviewed this book and some of the lessons I originally wrote were dramatically changed! I thought, "ohhh no no no, this is not trauma-informed. Let's change this!" and then I thought, "wow, look how far I've come!" To be able to recognize this, redirect, and admit I have learned better and am now dedicated to doing better is success in itself. There is no shame in that, but rather, pride in that! I'm glad I took a moment to review the person I was because it gave me context as to how much I've done to become the person I am today. I can't wait to look back 2 years from now!

- THE TIMELINE IS NOT IN YOUR CONTROL: Time is an illusion. A concept designed that makes us feel like we have some sort of control, but truly, we don't. We never know how much time we have in our lives, and every moment that passes is one you won't get back. Time waits for no one. Whether you are ready or not, it passes and brings you experiences meant to change you and teach you. You can learn from the timeline, but you cannot control it.

Living your life worried about the end results should tell you that you haven't healed from whatever lesson you needed to learn. Worrying about the future means you haven't learned to release control of situations. You're still trying to manipulate the outcome in some way. When is this going to come? Is it coming sooner? How can I reach my goals faster? Always about the end results. Have we learned nothing? If you only focus on the end result, you won't immerse yourself in the process and that end result you are looking for will always evade you.

Time to stop worrying about the timeline and start thinking about the here and now. This is where the magic happens; the lessons, cause and effect, what history is repeating, and what have we learned from it? To get to the future, we must reflect and learn from the past to avoid repeating our mistakes. Learning from them, criticizing them, and seeing the beauty in them.

This is something we all struggle with. "When will this happen?", "When will we be able to retire?", "When can we get to the weekend?" Even small things like driving to the store and being anxious to get there and get home rather than enjoying the experience and seeing what you can learn from it. Every interaction with another person, place, or animal, is something we can reflect on and learn from.

When I moved recently, Jazzy came with me, and Shaobear obviously stayed with Z and he was Z's pup. I knew the dogs would be sad, but I didn't realize how much they truly loved each other. Jazzy and Shaobear have gotten into kerfuffles in the past. A fight here, a bite there, mainly over toys or miscommunication. Bless Jazzy's little heart, but she can be quite oblivious to obvious cues. But when I took Shaobear to my apartment the week after we moved, Jazzy walked right up to him and gave him a big kiss. I actually caught it on video, and I replay it every so often. I took a moment to reflect on this and thought to myself, we don't deserve dogs; they teach us so many lessons. To think that regardless of the fights and bloodshed, these two little beings still love and protect each other and are able to forgive. Had I not been present, I would have missed that moment, that message, and that lesson. Don't get so caught up in chasing the future, that you forget to be present and witness those important moments.

Chapter 11

October 24, 2019, 9:50 pm

Thinking about the friends I have vs. the friends I want. Thinking about the two types of friends; unconditional and conditional.

Conditional friends: These are the ones who only want to be around for the good times. There are two types of conditional friends:

a. The selfish friends who are jealous or envious but pretend not to be. These friends don't want to listen to your problems, but always come to you with theirs.

b. The self-love/good vibes only friends who don't want any negative energy and don't want any kind of inconvenience in their lives because that hurts their "happiness". These individuals stay away from any real, uncomfortable topic but just because you avoid or ignore it, doesn't mean it's not there or won't affect you somehow. These friends will cut you off when you are going through tough times because it inconveniences them, or when you try to discuss real and difficult issues because it doesn't fit their toxic positivity. These friends may seem self-aware and mature and centered, but they aren't. Why? Because with maturity and growth comes maturity in relationships and this means understanding conflict, healthy boundaries, understanding that life isn't always all positivity and knowing that strong conflict resolution techniques are essential to healthy communication, growth and healthy relationships. It also means emotional growth and that comes with understanding the necessity in feeling and processing all emotions.

The unconditional friend: this is the one who has got your back and supports you 100%. This kind of friend realizes that no one is perfect, that people go through things, and this is normal. These friends understand that life holds negative and positive times, and that all vibes are welcome, even negative ones because those vibes don't last, and they teach us very important lessons about ourselves. These are the friends that aren't afraid to disagree, approach difficult topics, communicate, listen and grow with you.

During my separation with N and the trial, some of my friends really showed their true colours. They offered help without me asking, and then turned away when it came to doing what they said they would. When it came to helping me, to actually truly being there for me, they weren't around. The reason? Partly because they felt inconvenienced, partly because their offer was only performative an partly because of toxic, narcissistic traits they possessed. When it came to doing the right thing, standing up for injustice, being a true-blue friend, they decided to bail. This got me thinking, "what if everyone did this?", "What if everyone bailed because doing the right thing can be hard or difficult at times?", "What if every person decided not to get involved when it matters the most?"

- When someone is abused?

- When someone is wronged by the police?

- When someone is a victim of multiple crimes?

- When that victim is your friend?

What if no one stood up to say "NO! That's wrong! That cannot go unpunished!"

What then?

What would happen? To the world? To the just? To Humanity? To morals and ethics? To hopes and security? To integrity?

What are the kinds of friends I want in my life? What are the kinds of people I want in my world?

Unconditional friends. Friends who understand that a strong friendship is an ongoing relationship, and a relationship is not only positive and good times. There will be conflict and disagreements to work through and grow and learn from. But if this is a relationship that is important to both of you, you'll both be comfortable and feel safe in the knowledge that you have each other's back through thick and thin. Not in some ways, but in all ways, especially when it counts the most! Those are the friends that I want in my life.

Lessons:

- "THE ONLY WAY TO HAVE A FRIEND IS TO BE A FRIEND" – Ralph Waldo Emerson: This is one of my favourite quotes and a good one to live by. I started losing friends on my journey from being in and exiting the relationship with N. I lost a lot of friends when they turned and offered their opinion on how I should heal, and I disagreed. When I disagreed with their methods, they used it as their cue to bail on our friendship all together. This only proved to me that they weren't there to care, they simply wanted to control my process. Yes, I had a care package sent when I was locked up at home afraid to leave my house, but where were my friends? Thank you for sending soup, a word search and a yoga mat, but what I needed was support real support. People who were willing to be present and only a few people were.

When the same friends had a crisis, I dropped everything to help. Rides from the bus station an hour away, rides to work which was an hour and 15 mins away (one way) which meant an almost 3 hours round trip. I never said no. Anything they needed, I was there. That's what a friend is. That's the kind of friend I would want. When other friends needed me to lie for them, I did. When other friends needed me to cover for them, I did. Even to my own detriment. Even if they were wrong and the outcome was losing other friends and long-time connections. Anything my friends needed, I was there. I had no boundaries and did anything to prove I was a good friend. Even to my own detriment. I would put my friends before anything! To my old self, this was proving myself. To my new self, this is seeking validation. I wanted so badly to have a friend who would do as much for me as I would for them. And yet, during the most traumatic time in my life, the most difficult healing journey of my existence, distance. That's when I asked myself, "WHY on earth am I fighting so hard for people that wouldn't fight for me? People who are ok with disposing of me so easily when I no longer am convenient to them or fit their lifestyle?". This reminds me of my relationship with N. Doing so much and getting back nothing. I realized then that this was not just a pattern with my romantic relationships, but all relationships. This is why I had Narcissistic best friends and most of my boyfriends were toxic! Were they the issue? Yes. But so was I! Somehow, I learned that my value was directly related to what I had to offer. So, I always overextended myself because I learned, and was showed through friends and boyfriends, my childhood, and the system I grew up in, that I had to always be of service to be of value. But here is the kicker, your value doesn't come from what you can give, it comes from who you are as a person. The ones that only value what you can do are not your tribe, and there is no need to work so hard to keep them. They simply reinforce and keep you in the unhealed version of yourself. If people are meant to be in your life, they will truly love you through all your phases, they will stick by your side, value your growth, and want to grow with you.

Case and point, my friend Michelle. Yes, she is the one I acknowledged at the beginning of this book. We became close like sisters in the most unorthodox way. We've been the closest of friends so many years. She has supported me through my healing, my growth or lack thereof at times, and never deserted me. Even when we disagreed, even when we didn't see eye to eye, we respected each other and still supported each other. 3 months into knowing her, she proved to be a better friend than some friends I've known my entire life. My point? Don't try to cling to those people simply because you've known them for a long time. Nostalgia is a powerful emotion and will keep you tied to people who aren't meant for you. Let them go with love. If they grow and find a way to meet you where you are, then great! If they don't, they aren't meant to come with you on the abundant journey you are about to embark on. This is Source's way of protecting you. Once you let them go, amazing people will enter. Truly amazing people who will vibe with you and be on your level. Remember, boundaries with people or even removing people from your circle is for your own mental and emotional health and growth, and is a form of self-care, and self-care is not selfish, it's necessary.

- HAVE INTEGRITY: Stand up for what is right and what you believe in. Use your voice, even if you find yourself standing alone. Hold yourself and others accountable for their actions.

If a friend came to me for help, and I turned her down because it would inconvenience me, what would that say about me? That I would rather turn away from a friend in need that be inconvenienced? That my word to a friend means nothing? That it is ok for people to be wronged as long as it is not yourself? What would that mean for everything you stand for? Your morals? Your values? And what if everyone did the same? How many people would be wronged? How much injustice would go unpunished?

The issue with this mentality is, it allows history to repeat itself. It allows misinformation and misrepresentation, it allows actions to go unaddressed and unresolved and breeds resentment and passive aggressiveness or even worse, indifference. If we keep quiet over wrongdoing because we worry about what other people think, we have to start asking ourselves, why do we worry about what others think? If that's the case, analyze the fact that your friends won't be supportive of something you are passionate about and what does that say about the company you keep? Are they aligned with you? Your values and ethics? Time means nothing, character means everything! You can be better and closer friends with someone you've known for 2 weeks than someone you've known for 20 years.

I never thought I'd see the world in the kind of state it became during the pandemic. It's almost as if we regressed 60 years instantly! It was alarming! What was most alarming and disheartening was realizing some of the people whom I valued, really didn't share in the moral values I did. True colours started to show, real ethics and values (or lack thereof) started to seep out, and I took note of those who stayed quiet during times of crisis. To be silent is to be complicit in the harm that is perpetrated not only to

118

yourself and those around you but around the world. We are all connected as a global energetic collective and must remember this.

From Covid to the BLM movement to abortion rights, LGBTQ2A+ rights, to women being able to dance in public without a hijab in Iran, to the war in Ukraine, we see the world both regressing and progressing. Those who benefit from the regression sit quiet while the marginalized and disenfranchised scream at the tops of their lungs for help, reform, change.

I remember going to the BLM march and I had my signs ready to go, and a guy I was interested in at the time came over, looked at the sign and snickered. Later that evening he told me he saw me on the news and told his mom he knew me. The old me would have thought nothing of it, but the new me was very aware of the hypocrisy. He snickered at the cause, the idea, the issue but when it came to seeing someone he knew in the media, he claimed the attachment as some form of self-importance. Immediately I knew that he no longer fit in my life. We had great conversations, but when it came down to it, our core values did not align. I could pretend it didn't bother me, but that would be masking and performative and that goes against the grain of my soul, and I will not play small or sacrifice the growth I have made for anyone. Being true to myself is part of my growth and part of my healing and I need to respect and honour that.

This is the time to reflect: who are you, what do you stand for and how do you protect it? Who supports you? And who doesn't?

- WEED OUT YOUR LIFE JUST LIKE YOU WOULD YOUR GARDEN: Pay close attention to what you plant and what you nurture and be aware that this garden is where you will pluck what you need to sustain life. This garden IS your life source and what you grow and nurture feeds your mind, your heart and your soul. This garden is the sustenance, lessons, direction you set, and the example you pass on to others. It is what you live by. Ensure it is lively, strong, tended to, and beautiful. Weed it as necessary, feed it as necessary and let it be as necessary. Know when to let it grow, and when to dig up the old roots and start over again. Not everything will work out, but if you leave it unattended, what is rotting will affect the rest of the garden. It will take the energy and life force for whatever it has left and leave the rest stunted from their actual potential. You are the company you keep, the ideas you share and the conversations you engage in. These all shape your mind and affect your energy and requires attention.

For example, I used to have a job where the management team was problem-based. Every single time there was an issue, and someone made a suggestion it became some lengthy back and forth about how this won't work and that won't work, and this won't work. The focus was on why solutions aren't going to work rather than what could. What can we do that will work? What can we try for a short period and then re-evaluate? Those meetings took so much energy out of me that I would check out 15 minutes in. Imagine you are surrounding yourself with those types of individuals. Problem-based individuals. For every solution offered, they find a reason why it won't work and shut it all down without providing an alternative or a plan. It's exhausting. Those people don't want solutions or suggestions. They want to remain with the broken and just complain about it. It was poison for my mind. Naturally, I quit that job and moved on and as soon as I did, it felt like a massive weight was lifted! My anxiety calmed, and my nervous system settled. It was hard to imagine that someone's energy, even over zoom, was able to affect me mentally, emotionally, and physically in such a negative way. This is a perfect example of how you take on the energy of the company you keep and as we mentioned, negative energy is much more infectious than positive energy. It is now your duty to be aware, and mindful of who you keep in your inner circle and whether or not they are meant for your life in your current position. If they aren't, that's ok. That's their prerogative. You can't make someone grow if they aren't ready, nor do we have any right to try to tell them how, or when they should, so let them go with love. Guaranteed someone or something on the same level as you will come in. You cannot expect blessings from every new stage in life if you aren't ready to let go of what you have outgrown.

- "BE THE CHANGE YOU WISH TO SEE IN THE WORLD" – GHANDI: Truly, be the example. If no one is the example, step up and be that person. Don't be afraid of your light, don't hide in the shadows because that is what you have historically done or have been taught to do. You are not that person anymore; you are growing into the person you want to become and what will require you to do things you have never done. This means getting comfortable with being uncomfortable! Approaching difficult subjects, having difficult conversations and modeling the behaviour you want to see. We do not grow in our comfort zone. It takes us pushing ourselves, stepping up and stepping out. Doing the hard work that people don't want to attempt. Holding ourselves accountable just as we hold others accountable and be willing to say, "I was wrong, and I am dedicated to doing better." Learn from others and thank them for their lessons. Be the kind of human being you want to have in the world. Let's work on becoming the person we believe the world needs more of. Let's be the friend that we wish to have. Let's keep our expectations and standards high and hold people accountable while also holding ourselves accountable. And if people falter, help them up. No one is perfect and we all make mistakes, and usually make the same ones over again.

I used to always learn my lessons the hard way; but the harder the lesson to see, the more valuable it is! Just remember, just because someone does a bad thing, doesn't make them a bad person, and the opposite is also true. Just because someone does a nice thing, doesn't mean they are a nice person. Case and point: N did a lot of nice things for other people, always for some ulterior motive though.

Don't crucify people for making the same mistakes over again, help them learn from it. Give them love, help them remove that shame and guilt; the two things that eat at our soul and breed toxicity.

If there is no example to follow, be that example. Create that role model. Always heal to help heal.

Chapter 12

November 18, 2019

October and November have been life-changing for me. A serious game-changer. I shaved my head and embraced it. I stopped wearing my wig every day and just go out with my baldness. I still get looks and stares but I'm ok with it because I'm ok with me. Will I wear my wig to the trial? Yes. Will I wear my wig to the awards gala tomorrow? Maybe. But not because I am hiding, but because I want to and it's cute. I received such overwhelming support from my family and friends when I decided to post to the world about my hair issues and why I decided to shave my head. I was bleaching my hair to make the bald spots less noticeable because I am still slightly self-conscious about it, but the fact that I can go about my day without a problem is such a game-changer.

I'm living up to my own standards of beauty and not society's constructed standards of what beauty is. I keep my morals high and my ethics close to my heart. I hold others to the same moral standards I hold myself to, and that has:

1. Changed my social circle.

2. Weeded out those who weren't good for me.

The true sign of growth is when you are ok with the wrong people exiting your life. But I digress. Back to my hair, or more importantly, what it, or lack of it, represents. Let's call it my baldness. Even though my hair is (almost) fully growing back, I call my stubble head, bald.

My baldness represents strength.

My baldness represents self-awareness.

My baldness represents growth.

My baldness represents morals and values.

My baldness represents power.

My baldness represents confidence.

My baldness represents a new chapter in my life.

My baldness represents hope.

Most importantly, my baldness represents the me I have always wanted to become but never had the ability to shine through. It represents moving forward and being fulfilled as a person, as an individual. Letting go of all the past traumas and toxic experiences and finally becoming the person I was meant to be.

I always struggled with the old adage, "everything happens for a reason". To be honest, every so often, I find myself still skeptical. I do, however, believe that the universe throws us challenges, and we are offered a choice. I was a victim. I was traumatized. I could have chosen to stay in the victim role and let that define me, as many people do, but instead, I let that build me!

I lost my hair and learned to accept my afflictions and grow from them. I was pushed to a traumatic breaking point to force me into therapy to grow as a person. I was victimized in order to push me to find and reveal my true identity and to find ways to heal from trauma. My identity, however, is not that of a victim but one of a survivor.

A Thriver.

A Believer.

A Builder.

A stronger, more aware version of what I was. Of course, I have so much more growing to do but this is just the beginning of a new life.

Now that I know who I am and am comfortable with who I am, I can truly become better. I can welcome change rather than fear it or fight it. I can welcome growth in its many abstract forms rather than fight it. I can truly learn to swim with the tide rather than swim against it. I do not fear the future. I welcome it. Because I know that I am going to live and learn, and if I can survive all that has happened, I can get through anything with this new outlook.

What helped? What did I do?

- I told people. I shared my story rather than hide it and got such positivity and support back.

- I helped people whom I had no idea were struggling by sharing my story, and I found my purpose.

- I used social media and followed people that were going through struggles and found strength in community.

- I accepted myself and all my flaws.

- I stopped judging myself.

- I held myself accountable for my actions, thoughts, and words and held others accountable for theirs.

Doing that was a game-changer y'all! Putting yourself first and dedicating yourself to self-growth. Understanding your part in the process and your part in the problem is so important. You do have to check yourself. Your thoughts, your actions, your words, your values, your morals, your part in the problem, and your part in the resolution.

Check… your….self.

Improve… your… self!

Working towards a better version of yourself is part of checking yourself. Understand your flaws and insecurities and work hard on addressing what the root cause is to give attention and heal those tears in your fabric. Understand others in the process and understand how fear and insecurity play into their shortcomings and this will lend to understanding others and taking responsibility to end the cycle, rather than spending your time blaming everyone else for your problems.

Did my ex do me wrong? Yes.

Is he responsible for me feeling how I do? Partly. I am responsible for how I feel.

Is it my job to change my perspective and rebuild? Absolutely!

No one can do this for me. I know that. No one can make me feel a certain way if I don't let them.

That is me taking responsibility and, more importantly, me taking your power back.

I am powerful!

Lessons:

- BE TRUE TO YOURSELF: There is a saying I live by, "You are nothing if not truly genuine". Harsh perhaps, but true. I remember this day, the moment I decided to go and shave my head. The day I had enough of hiding and the stress it caused, the anxiety it caused.

Since I was 13, I'd go through spurts where I would lose a small dime or a quarter-sized patch of hair here or there. Then it would grow back. I'd lose it again. Then it would grow back. I lived in constant shame. Styling it in high school was the hardest. Some years I would go without putting it up because of where the hair loss was. One year I wore a bandana the entire year because nothing else could hide it. I remember being so nervous for Prom because I didn't know what I was going to do with my hair! So, my mom took me to a hairdresser who managed an updo that covered my spot. But the real and most extreme hair loss happened when the abuse worsened with N and I lost so much hair that I was panicking and the more I panicked, the more I lost until I simply was unable to hide it anymore. I had lost almost half my hair. I confided in my mom and once again, she took me to a hairdresser that cut it all off into a pixie cut, and then my mom got me a wig. I hid under that for an entire year until I was fed up.

When I shaved my head, someone commented, "it's liberating isn't it?" And I struggled with that. Was it liberating? Without my wig, without hair, I got a lot of looks and some backlash. And when my hair started to grow back patchy, even more so. I remember going to breakfast with my parents one morning and people in the diner kept staring. Here and there I would get compliments from people that liked my look; my glasses paired with my earring and bold lipstick which I used to compensate for my baldness. I also started dressing the way I wanted to, not the way people expected me to. Was it liberating? No. It wasn't. I felt like people actually boxed me in even more. I was subject to insults constantly. I was called a "Dyke" often. Some people said I was trying to look like a man. When my hair was growing back, some people said I was too old for "that kind of cut" and I should stop trying to be young. I was more accepted when I dressed like everyone else and wore my wig. But I'll tell you what the freeing experience was. It was when I realized I've been through worse than whatever judgement people had to project. Instead of walking with my head down, I walked with it up. If people stared at me, I'd smile rather than cower. If people looked at my head, I'd run my fingers over my head to bring attention to it rather than hide it. I dove headfirst into being and accepting where I was in the moment, rather than anxiously waiting for the day my hair grew back.

That was a freeing and liberating moment. Not shaving my head, but the journey to realizing who I was without my hair and freeing and liberating myself from the opinions of others. My hair literally comes and goes. It does not make, break or define me. My looks will fade one day and I'm fully aware of that. To this day I still pull out and lose my hair. Some people smoke when stressed, some ppl cry when overwhelmed, I lose my hair. My body will literally tell me that I am stressed long before I realize it. This is why it is so important to prioritize self care and understand what are your triggers, where is your stress threshold and how to manage. Stress is a toxin, a poison, but also necessary to trigger growth, self reflections, understanding urgency and it's unavoidable. What you need to focus on are the stressors that you can control and how to manage those. The stressors you can't control will be there regardless of whether or not you stress about it/them. Learn to pick and choose your battles wisely.

- WHAT HAPPENED TO YOU DOES NOT DEFINE YOU: When bad things happen, it's really easy to get sucked into the victim role. To feel like being a victim is your identity. You define yourself by the incident. But that is not who you are! You were victimized, but you are not forever a victim. You are strong and brave, and resilient. You are beautiful and aware and confident. That is your identity. That is who you are. It's easy to lose yourself in the grief and sorrow but do not let it consume you and become a martyr.

What happens when you get stuck in the victim role, is, you lose who you are, your real identity and you become the incident, the trauma and revictimize yourself over and over again. You are a survivor, but that is only part of your identity. That is only but a fraction of what has shaped you and taught you valuable lessons. There are so many other facets of your being that are equally as important.

We are not our mistakes; we are our decisions moving forward. This ties into letting go of the shame or the guilt. These emotions are what keep us chained to the event rather than flying with the lessons we learned. When you are stuck in the incident, in the victim mentality, you are stunting your own growth, you are not allowing yourself to truly and fully learn from your trauma because you are tying your identity to it. Your past and your mistakes do not define your future self. Every small, conscious decision you make moving forward does. Every right decision, every empathetic thought, the kindness you lead with. Those are the new bricks and building blocks to use to build on. That is your new solid foundation. That is what defines who you are.

Chapter 13

November 24th, 2019, 3:03 pm

I was thinking about kindness and forgiveness yesterday.

People talk about forgiveness as something that is necessary for healing, as something that you need to do for yourself to heal.

As I'm sitting down to write this, the song from Selena Gomez "Lose you to love me," comes on. Maybe a sign? Anyways, I always wondered about this forgiveness concept. I thought a lot about it because I question if I can forgive him and what he did. The fact that I question this makes me believe I can't forgive him. This doesn't mean I can't fully heal, does it? I don't like the thought of that my healing depends on him being forgiven, on him gaining forgiveness.

Maybe the concept of forgiveness and forgiving is actually about forgiving myself, not necessarily him.

Maybe that is the forgiveness we truly require to heal. Maybe that is the real meaning.

I think only God can forgive my ex for the things that he has done. I can't forgive such terrible things done to someone. How do you forgive abuse? Intentionally hurting someone and breaking them down? How do you forgive such things from a person who knew he did wrong but doesn't care? Or even worse, doesn't even realize what he did wrong? Nor does that person care for your forgiveness.

What I can do is forgive myself for having allowed it to happen and forgiving myself for having allowed it to continue. I forgive myself for my lack of judgement and bad decisions that were guided by unhealed trauma and an unprotected and unaddressed hurt and traumatized inner child. An inner child that should have healed and been protected. All those traumas that I should have understood and addressed. I forgive myself for that.

I forgive myself for not believing in myself. For setting the bar for the respect I received, so low. For not putting myself first and not listening to my gut instinct. For not respecting myself enough to love myself enough to set the bar high. To set an expectation of the kind of respect I will receive and not fail myself.

I forgive myself for that.

I am also thankful. I am not thankful for what happened; how can anyone be thankful for a terrible situation? But what I am thankful for is the lessons this situation has taught me. I am thankful for the balance I have now, not in spite of what happened but because of what happened. I am thankful for the person I have become.

A more aware person.

A stronger person.

A braver person.

Someone who needed help but was unable to find it until now.

I am no longer dependent. I am now an emotionally independent person.

I am healthy and strong mentally and emotionally and that reflects physically.

I was thinking of how I would feel testifying in court in front of him. I know I'll have nerves. That's a given. I wouldn't be human if I didn't. However, I won't let him scare me or intimidate me anymore. He can only do that if I give him that power, and I won't do that.

Does it hurt to relive what happened? Yes.

What he did was terrible, and it hurt. It cost me a lot. My family, my friends, my mental health, my physical health, my baby boy; but I am powerful now.

I am no longer a victim. I was a victim, then I was a survivor, and now I'm a thriver.

Now I am strong. Now I am powerful, and I am taking my power back. He cannot hurt me unless I allow him to, and I will no longer allow him that kind of control or power. No one can make me feel any type of way unless I let them. He is not someone I will allow to control how I feel anymore because I do not care what he thinks. That does not matter.

I matter.

Lessons:

- HEALING AND GROWTH IS NOT A LINEAR JOURNEY: Wow. It is truly shocking how much I healed, then regressed back to the unhealed version of myself, and then healed again since first writing this. You know that old saying, "two steps forward and one step back"? Such is healing. It can be a frustrating journey. One moment you feel great, and the next, you are reacting to triggers you thought you once healed. Then you heal that trigger and feel great and another one pops up. Just like that onion we spoke about earlier. Even years later, you may find yourself in a situation that you didn't realize was triggering and there you go, reacting vs. responding again. Reacting out of hurt rather than responding with love and empathy.

It happens to the best of us. Reading that entry makes me take a good hard look at the past few years. Where was I, where did I end up and why am I here now? I thought I had quit those codependent ways, searching for validation and begging for someone to love me. Well, I was when I was single. The true test is the next relationship you enter into. That is what is really going to test your growth.

Was my growth tested? Like you wouldn't believe! I entered a new relationship and the same patterns emerged. I invested everything I had into him, and neglected me and my passions. Like I mentioned before, this book went by the wayside. I gave up on my hobbies and tried to manage and cater to his healing and gave up on mine. What happened? Source took away all the things I worked so hard for. Because I worked so hard to get those things for someone else, not myself. I had all the lessons, I did all the homework, and then I walked right into the test and failed hard. I let myself get triggered, reacted rather than responded, stopped practicing my mantras, stopped therapy, thought I was all good, and clearly, I wasn't. The house we bought, the business I helped grow, all taken away. To say I felt devastated and betrayed is an understatement. Like I mentioned, when Source teaches me a lesson, it's usually a big one.

The trauma all that put me through was intense, and mimicked what I had gone through with N. My brain understood the person and situation was different, but my body experienced the stress and trauma in the same way. It spurred me right back into healing. I started seeing my trauma therapist weekly. I was spending time with myself, by myself, doing things I loved. I dove back into my spirituality. I started going back to Church, I connected with Source, started taking classes again, quit toxic jobs, and left it up to Source to figure it out while I worked on the things that I had let fall by the wayside. What a lesson, what a wake-up call, what a realization.

It's easy to get down on ourselves when times get hard, and we are inclined to blame the other party or parties, but we, as discussed, have a large role to play, and it is our responsibility to reflect on what that is. So, here's to breaking old cycles (again) and being aware and vigilant that people and situations do not influence you and push you to revert back to the unhealed version of yourself. We may fall, we may falter, but we will not revert to that unhealed self. We will keep growing and learning.

- LEARN WHAT FORGIVENESS MEANS TO YOU: This is a tough one. It took me years to really discover what forgiveness meant to me, and I told Kathy about this a couple of months ago. There are so many reasons people list off when they feel you should forgive and I'm sure most of them are great, but forgiveness is only performative if you don't truly know what it means to you.

What does forgiveness mean to me? Well, let me tell you a story to help add context. Years ago, when I was in my early 20s, I had a good friend, like a cousin, who was a victim of a violent home invasion. He later passed of an unrelated event and it was devastating.

Years later, I mean this year, in 2023, I would come face to face with one of the individuals I thought was one of the perpetrators (Admittedly, I was wrong and misinformed and held onto that misinformation for decades due to my own bias and trauma). I hadn't seen this individual in over a decade, and when I did, I had such mixed feelings. I got home (I was still living at my house at the time) and I was doing my dishes, almost meditating, and I got a message from my cousin to forgive. Sounds crazy right? Well not really. I am a medium and I receive messages regularly. But this one, I was shocked. And then it hit me, if he, in the afterlife, can forgive, who am I to hold on to the anger and hate? If the person that was victimized says to forgive, who am I to go against that advice? The next day I saw that individual again, and I started having an inner dialogue with myself. If he says to forgive, what right do I have to deny? And who am I to judge if this person is worthy of forgiveness or not? If that individual was sorry, who am I to determine what level of sorry is sorry enough to warrant forgiveness and who am I to put such a high price on forgiveness? So, I forgave. I didn't approach, I didn't say anything out loud, but I allowed myself to say, "I forgive". When I got home that night and was talking to Z about the entire experience, I stated crying. I got so emotional that I broke down into tears. All that anger, all that resentment, all that hate that I held onto, it was gone. That heavy rock in my heart when I thought about the situation, gone. It was almost like I had this existential release of whatever emotion I had kept inside for decades.

I learned that forgiveness wasn't for anyone else. Forgiving someone didn't mean I had to be friends with them or allow them back into my life, or even like them for that matter. Forgiveness meant releasing the emotions I had tied to that person, that situation, that event. To me, forgiveness meant that I would not longer hold onto that pain, that anger. I was able to release it. Forgiveness wasn't tied to them, it was tied to me. To my emotions. And once I was able to forgive, it helped me release those emotions. To forgive didn't mean I had to be cordial, civil, or even provide any energy their way. It simply meant that I would not carry that pain with me any longer.

I also want to note that forgiveness is not necessary to move forward. It is a personal choice for you and you only. Sometimes, the best thing you can do is walk away, and understand that the person is, and will stay toxic and if you feel good already, you don't need to forgive. Not being able to forgive doesn't mean you aren't growing, and forgiving doesn't necessarily signal growth.

- THE ABUSE YOU ENDURED IS NOT EXCLUSIVE TO YOU: This is such an important point. Abuse is like a spider web. It starts with you, but then slowly touches everyone around you. When you go through something as dark and traumatic as narcissistic abuse, it's easy to get caught up in the "you don't understand" mentality. But remember, you are not the only one affected by the abuse.

When you are in an abusive relationship, you are prone to be very sensitive to people's energies, you are hypervigilant with tones and demeanors, you internalize everything, and your anxiety is through the roof. You may have an awful reaction to simple things because your nervous system is off-key. Not only that but then there are the events, the outings, and being with your friends. Always worried about how the Narc will behave, what they will say, are they going to try to trigger you while you're out? If you go out and s/he has fun, are you going to be able to leave or if you ask to leave are they going to get mad?

Then there's the lying, and missing special events because Narcissists tend to ruin special events. I can't count how many times

I either cancelled events or went alone after a fight simply because of N. Right at the last minute, something would come up, or he'd pick a fight just before and I'd cancel it all or lie to excuse his absence.

You may also be short with your friends and family, more prone to getting triggered, getting defensive. You may even take on toxic traits yourself because you are exposed to it so much in your personal life. You may also be short with co workers. You may be doing poor work, unable to focus or concentrate, unable to even go to work because of arguments that lasted all night long. And let's not forger that the Narcissist likely fooled your family and friends as well. They too will experience the hurt and betrayal. It's important to keep this in mind so you can support your support system just as they support you.

Take my parents for example. My parents are the strongest people I know – bless them, I can't thank them enough for standing by me through all my nonsense. Like the almost full year I went without speaking to them because N had convinced me they were bad people, and he was the only person there for me. When I turned to them the morning after the police came, they never even hesitated to help. The amount of hurt they endured due to him was immense as well. My father, I'd never seen him cry before this. My mother even cancelled her 9 week trip to Malaysia so she could be there to support me during the trial. I can't imagine how difficult it must have been to sit there and listen to my testimony. I remind myself every day that the trauma I endured didn't only affect me, it affected everyone around me. The entire relationship was filled with me crying to my parents, them seeing my hurt, them dealing with his nonsense. They also had gone through the manipulation and narcissistic abuse with me. On top of that pain, my parents endured the added pain of someone manipulating and stealing away their daughter.

My friends, the ones that stood by me also were victims of residual trauma. The ones that listened patiently, kept giving me the same advice over and over again like a broken record, hoping I would come to my senses. They endured the abuse too. When I was short, when I was anxious, when I was reactive, all because of what was going on at home. They endured all that as well.

Not only does this affect friends and family, but we need to be mindful when the next relationship comes around. When I started dating, I didn't realize how much I still needed to work out. But getting into another relationship showed me that although I was ok on my own, I was still unhealed when it came to love. I didn't know what unconditional love was and was still trying to figure it out. I didn't realize how many new triggers would arise and I struggled through them. Not only was I managing his triggers, but I was also trying to manage mine, and things broke down. I didn't just jump into another relationship either. I worked on myself and took a long time to heal. N and I ended in 2018, and I didn't jump into another relationship until 2020. I didn't realize then how much my trauma would spill over into my new relationship. I also put too much responsibility on him to watch for triggers, to keep from triggering me, and to understand when he did. But that's such an impossible task. It is not the responsibility of others to manage your triggers. Yes, your support system needs to know about your journey to help you through it, but we are responsible for our own healing journey and managing ourselves. I also didn't explain what I had endured. He understood my ex was a Narcissist, but I never went into any detail about the trauma and abuse I endured. I wasn't open about it, I didn't want to talk about it and therefore gave him no context.

I'm not going to say, "until you are healed, stay out of a relationship" because who am I to decide when you are ready? I didn't even know when I was ready. But the one thing I can say is this, your partner is there to support you, love you without condition, not be the one on the receiving end of your trauma responses. Having open and honest conversations about your past is essential to anyone, especially your partner, knowing why you are the way you are and to understand that you are on a healing journey as well. This will allow space to talk, learn how to communicate, and argue/disagree in a healthy and constructive, not destructive manner.

Remember, healing is not only healing yourself but also allowing the space for others to heal as well. Giving all those relationships just as much love, healing, attention, and grace you gave yourself during your healing process.

Chapter 14

December 7th, 1:04 pm

Watching my kitten play with a piece of paper towel on the floor and I think to myself "Look how much fun Beans is having with that tiny piece of paper towel". Bouncing and flying through the air. I can buy him the most expensive cat toys but he prefers this tiny piece of paper towel.

It reminds me that it's the little things in life you have to appreciate and be thankful for. Those things are just as precious. We get so preoccupied with what society tells us we should value that we forget that we should really take a hot minute to stop and value the smaller things or the free things or the things that we take for granted on a regular day.

Great weather.

A visit from a friend.

A spare moment to sip tea and reflect.

The love you receive from your family.

Your health.

That you love yourself and put yourself first.

Fresh air and nice walks.

The way your pets look at you with unconditional love.

The sound of a baby's laughter.

Right now, my dog is giving me those puppy dog eyes and I could be so annoyed that she is going to leave drool on my jeans but instead, I am thankful that I have her unconditional love and adoration.

It's all about perspective.

<u>**Lessons:**</u>

- PERSPECTIVE IS EVERYTHING. Changing your perspective will essentially change your life. You must lessen your stress and that comes from reframing your perspective on situations and events. When you sweat the small stuff, you will attract the same negativity you project. That same anxiety you are putting out. Worry only breeds worry and negativity. You don't have any control over the end result anyways.

Changing your perspective not only takes personal growth but requires a level of self-reflection, understanding, empathy and kindness. It's easy to be bias. It's easy to choose a side based on our conditioned selves. But you are not the conditioned self anymore, and you're proud of that! So now, how do you form your own perspective? What drives it?

It should be your heart. Lead with your heart. Don't be afraid to lead with love. Be strong enough to be vulnerable. We should always choose to lead with love, vulnerability and understanding. I feel as though it was a blessing to go through what I went through, and I can appreciate that now. Rather than the "why me" attitude, I adopted the "I know why me" perspective.

I know why things happened the way they did. In hindsight, I had so many traumas I needed to heal, so many issues I needed to figure out. I needed to find myself and love myself for who I was rather than continue finding emotionally unavailable people to earn love and affection from. Without this journey, these hardships, I wouldn't have found who I was truly meant to be. Without the mess with N, I would have never entered trauma therapy, which was necessary for me to address my traumas, not just from the relationship but the deeper issues that caused me to continue the pattern of abusive or toxic relationships.

You cannot heal if you don't admit there is a problem and you can't identify that problem until you take a step back, remove yourself from the victim mentality, alter that perspective, self reflect and hold yourself accountable.

- ENJOY THE SIMPLE THINGS IN LIFE: We seriously overcomplicate things in our lives. Maybe this stems from the socially constructed norm that being busy is good and if you're not busy you're lazy. Sitting and watching my cat play with a piece of paper rather than the toys I spent a fortune on reminds me that you don't need much to be happy, your just need good company, love and safety, and to remember the small things that brought and bring you pleasure.

I adopted those two little ones for Jazzy, to help her through the process, and in turn they gave me so much more. Watching their relationship build with Jazzy reminded me that there is nothing that prevents us from getting along other than ourselves. As long as we have a safe environment where we're able to be our true authentic self without judgement, we will flourish, grow and thrive! It also reminded me to take a moment and appreciate the small things we usually blow right past or see as inconveniences.

Remember when you were younger, and the small, simple things brought so much pleasure.

- The sound of the rain
- The first snowfall and flakes landing on your eyelashes
- Finding a dime or a feather on the floor
- The smell and sound of leaves crunching under your feet
- The warm feeling of the sun on your face

It's amazing how much stopping to think and appreciate the simple things can help heal. Not only does it force you to pause, but it forces you to clear your head. I like to think of this as a mini meditation break. It forces you to come back to the present, be present and be in the moment. Next time you are having a hard time, take a second, pause, and find something that you can focus on and ground yourself for just a few minutes before going about your day again. Just today, I was walking up the driveway and a Dove flew overhead. I took a second, watched it soar, smiled, and then continued on my way. Small moments like these can make such a big difference in your day. Take that moment to take a deep breath, cut whatever negative ties you have accrued over the day, and exhale that negativity back out.

Chapter 15

Jan 5, 8:25 pm

There I sit, trying to relax and write a chapter of my book, and I hear a couple fighting through my window. I listen for a minute, nervously, not trying to find out what they are fighting over but where it was coming from. Was it people on the street? The neighbours? The people in the building next door? Because I heard this last night too. Then my thoughts shift. I start wondering if this is what people felt like when they would hear N going off when he was mad. Jessica once told me that people in the high-rise two houses down used to be able to hear our fighting. One time she said she saw someone trying to climb the fence to get a better listen. I thought, "Is this what it's like?". Then I stopped thinking and started feeling. Feeling sad that this was how those neighbours must have felt. Like when Nikki from upstairs used to turn her TV down and listen, "just in case". Who was the person yelling, and are they both mad? Or is someone getting abused? I felt nervous. Like my anxiety was going and I was shaking my leg, and my hands were gripped together. I felt anxiety, like I was going to have an anxiety attack, just like when he used to yell at me. Then I had an AH HA! moment. I began to think again. I began to process. I understood what was happening. PTSD. That was what was happening. But I won't let it control me. I let myself feel but was also able to identify why I was feeling that way, and address and process those feelings. I calmed myself down and closed the window, turned to my journal and started to write.

Lessons:

- BUILD: Build a community of inspired individuals by leading by example. Use the important lessons to help inspire others. Surround yourself with people that inspire you and make you want to do better and be better. People that encourage you, stimulate you, support you and hold you accountable.

My neighbours were always looking out for me without me knowing. The older French man in the building two houses down, my neighbours next door or even upstairs. I had no idea. I ran into the French man two buildings down one day and he told me that him and his son were keeping an eye on the parking lot, on my car, on my building because they knew. This man that I barely knew, was looking out for me. What a kind and caring thing to do. Observe and reflect on the company you keep and on the community you're a part of. I truly appreciate the small comments and acts that made me feel safe. It truly made such a huge difference.

I also started volunteering after N and I broke up. I found an organization that I loved and was passionate about and committed to them and became a part of that wonderful community. I made myself go to places alone if no one wanted or were able to go with me, and from there I'd meet new and interesting people. I expanded my horizons, tried new things, allowed new people into my life and things started flourishing and opportunities started to open up.

Put yourself back out there and build a community for yourself, the kind you've always dreamt about. Filled with encouraging, healthy and kind individuals committed to constant growth. Take classes, or read books, lots of books. Don't just build your community, build your mind, your talents, a business! Anything to flip the script and gain back a sense of self. Even if you find you don't like certain things, that's still a part of discovering yourself and an important part of your journey.

Do what lights your soul on fire but also brings your soul peace and happiness, and make sure it's not your job! I say this because we are so inclined to think. "If you do something you love, you never work a day in your life", but the issue is that people who have gone through trauma can become hyper focused on their tasks. If you are doing something you love for a living while you are new to your healing journey, it's easy to lose balance and become consumed with work. This is just another way we escape. If your hobby is your work, find another outlet for you to be able to decompress or you will burn out and lose that passion. When you turn your passion into work but don't have balance, that is all you will do, it will consume you. The stressors that come with running a business are heavy, and the last thing you want is for that to syphon the love out of what you do. Find an outlet for yourself where you can decompress and find balance.

Let's all help each other get through life. Life is hard enough as it is. Let's not make it any more difficult for yourself or the next person. Let's build a community, be a community and help each other thrive to be the best person they can be and leave a legacy that will inspire and motivate others to do the same.

- DON'T UNDERESTIMATE THE POWER OF HABIT: We are creatures of habit. We thrive on routine. I cannot stress the importance of routine. When you are trying to reregulate your nervous system, if you are like me, routine is your saviour. However, living with anxiety, change can be difficult for me. I try to let go of the outcome, but the flow needs to be in order for me to feel calm and focused. So, I created a routine. I wake up at the same time every day. I read, have my coffee, make my shake. Same routine every morning. I also go to bed at the same time every night to make sure I get my rest in. This helps me relax and get to the rest and digest stage.

One thing you need to know, is that the rest and digest stage can feel off if you've been living with trauma for a long time. It can feel dangerous or unsafe. If you are used to the chaos, this will make you uneasy. In these times, we are prone to self-sabotage, an unfortunate by-product of trauma. This is totally normal. Give it time and give yourself time to adjust. Don't give in just because "it doesn't feel right" because honestly, the reason we got into this situation in the first place is because our internal sensors are off. The silence, the calm, it will make you uncomfortable. Allow yourself the time to adjust and create that new habit.

You are allowed to have flaws. You are allowed to make mistakes. You are allowed to fail or feel uncomfortable, but you are NOT allowed to give up.

Chapter 16

February 19, 2020

When you wake up from your fog, and you feel like this new person, you want to go around and continuously tell people, "I'm not the same woman *[person]* I was 6 months ago" because you worked so hard to become the woman *[person]* you are today. And you are proud of her *[him]*. Like a kid who made their first piece of art or something. Like, just proud! So, you are happy to talk about what it's like to heal day by day!

So, you are happy to talk about that part of the healing. People love to talk about that part of the healing. No one talks about the awful parts. Like how horrible it is when you wake up from your fog, and you're embarrassed and ashamed of the woman *[person]* you were. The one you had become. No one talks about the humiliation of facing your friends, and the friends you lost. The anxiety and the shame. No one talks about that, only the fluffy stuff. Never the nights you cried yourself to sleep because you felt so ashamed. The crying because of all the bridges you burned. The people you hurt. The advice you never took and the frustration they must have felt. No one talks about all that. But it's important to talk about all of that.

That's part of the healing process. Healing isn't all revelations, epiphanies, and newfound self-awareness and awakenings. It's rough. It's difficult. It's hours of crying in your therapist's office. Hours of crying at home. The anger you have to learn to process and let go of. The shame and anxiety you have to learn to properly process and accept. It's reading books and watching videos on hard topics. It's doing your homework every single day in order to keep growing and gaining the tools you need in your arsenal to process the emotions that accompany any difficult situation. It's learning to set boundaries and identify traits that are toxic in yourself and others. It's coming to terms with your flaws, identifying them and trying to improve yourself through self-love and respect, wanting to be the best version of yourself that you can be. To thrive and attract and manifest good and positivity. It's truly raising those vibrations to level up! That's what those messy and distressing emotions build.

Don't be ashamed to feel. Every situation, positive and negative, brings a lesson.

Every lesson builds who you are.

This was all a step in a greater plan for you.

Have faith.

Lessons:

- THE GLOW-UP CAN BE LONELY: One thing I didn't take into consideration when I began this wild healing journey is how lonely it can be. Once you start to heal, discover your true self, and start seeing things for what they are rather than what you want them to be, your circle gets smaller.

Some people may not like this new healing version of yourself and make their exit. Herein lies the struggle. Nostalgia is a powerful thing. We hold on to people, places, and things because we have emotional attachments. Even when these things no longer have a place in our life, we make them fit. We hold on, and we rationalize it. I'm not the exception. I have a stuffed animal from when I was 3 years old. She's tucked away safely in my sock drawer. I have no use for her, I don't use her, and she's not out for display, but I'll cut my right arm off before I get rid of that sausage dog stuffed animal. The difference is that little stuffie isn't doing me any harm by being present. On the other hand, if you have a Narcissistic best friend or partner or family member, you now realize the type of person he or she is, and you hold onto them and their toxic energy simply because of the history you have together, this will prevent your growth and stunt your healing.

I'm not saying you need to cut people out of your life completely. This is where boundaries come in. Let them go with love or change your expectation of them and your relationship. It's not easy to do, especially if those people are family, but it is necessary for your growth and healing. Set boundaries, learn how to hold them, and understand that anyone who has an issue with your boundaries isn't worried about the boundary. They are worried about the control they are losing as a result of you setting boundaries. As the saying goes, "The only people who will get offended by you setting boundaries are the ones that benefitted from you not having any in the first place."

I'll tell you a secret though, once your make room in your life, the people aligned with your true self will fall right in. You need to clear what is no longer serving you in order to make room for what can and will. Make room for your soul tribe to come dancing in and take you to that next level. You also need to hold yourself accountable to your mistakes and the people you hurt along the way. I always say, people are in your life to love you, hurt you, heal you and teach you. You may be the subject of these people, and also be one of these people. Just because people have fallen out of your life, doesn't mean it was because they were the toxic ones; sometimes the issue is you. Learn to set that ego aside and ask for forgiveness just as you forgive others.

- DON'T COMPARE YOUR JOURNEY TO ANYONE ELSE'S JOURNEY: The start of your journey is the one that comes when you've finally found yourself, your path and your soul's true purpose. All the other starts were just false starts! Those races, won or not, were only practice and prep for the real deal. Our journeys only starts once we have finally figured out the lessons we need to learn to be ready for that final race. The race where you have the tools, you have the lessons, the wisdom, the inner truths, and true confidence to do it your way, not anyone else's.

My race started at 38! After repeating cycle after cycle, repeating the same mistakes, and not learning the lessons. Only after I discovered who I was, who I've been trying to be, and who I want to truly become, did things become clear. Things aren't perfect, but they are falling into place now and I can see and appreciate that.

It took a lot to stop trying to control the process. Not knowing what is coming up, how it's going to turn out, and what the path is, was enough to make me sick. I always needed a plan, a path, a route, and to know the potential outcome. I never lived in the present, and I started to realize that. Half the issues that I thought would happen probably wouldn't. And a ¼ of those were usually self-fulfilling prophesies. I learned to go back to living in the present. Being grateful and practicing gratitude. Learning to snap out of it, bring my mind back to the present, and not be so hard on myself when my mind wanders. I kiboshed the natural go-to mindset of lack, and I started being thankful for whatever abundance I had. A roof over my head, 2 sweet pups, and food in my belly. I started counting my blessings; parents that love me, my self-confidence, and a solid understanding of myself among other blessings. Bringing myself back to the present moment helped me learn to appreciate the process rather than be anxious about the possible and potential end result. It also helped me not care so much about the end result because I found ways to enjoy the process.

Do I know where I will be tomorrow? Probably at home, working on my book, but I'm not concerned about it. And if plans change, I'll change with them. I learned it's easier and much less damaging if you ride the wave rather than try to swim against it. That's also where the beautiful lessons lie.

YOU GOT THIS!

Resources:

1. The Neuroscience of Narcissism and Narcissistic Abuse by Shirley Davis | Jun 22, 2020 | CPTSD and Narcissistic Abuse, CPTSD Research | https://cptsdfoundation.org/2020/06/22/the-neuroscience-of-narcissism-and-narcissistic-abuse/#:~:text=Children%20of%20narcissists%20also%2C%20like,the%20lives%20of%20these%20children.

2. Long-Term Narcissistic Abuse Can Cause Brain Damage By Kim Saeed - Author, Researcher, Educator on October 20, 2017 https://psychcentral.com/blog/liberation/2017/10/long-term-narcissistic-abuse-can-cause-brain-damage#4

3. National Library of Medicine. Hippocampus in health and disease: An overview Kuljeet Singh Anand and Vikas Dhikav https://www.ncbi.nlm.nih.gov/pmc/articles/PMC3548359/#:~:text=Hippocampus%20is%20a%20complex%20brain,of%20neurological%20and%20psychiatric%20disorders.

4. Anatomy and Physiology of the Hippocampus Written by Michael A. Yassa https://www.britannica.com/science/hippocampus

5. Psychiatrist explains how the brain blocks memory to help get through traumatic event https://www.news-medical.net/news/20161209/Psychiatrist-explains-how-the-brain-blocks-memory-to-help-get-through-traumatic-event.aspx

6. Narcissistic personality disorder https://www.ncbi.nlm.nih.gov/books/NBK556001/

7. Medline drug information https://medlineplus.gov/druginfo/meds/a682053.html

8. NIH
   https://www.ncbi.nlm.nih.gov/books/NBK532890/

9. A broader view of psychopathy
   https://www.apa.org/monitor/2022/03/ce-corner-psychopathy

10. 15 Essential ways to practice self reflection
    https://www.minimalismmadesimple.com/home/self-reflection/

11. Lesson our emotions can teach us – and how we can learn.
    https://psychcentral.com/blog/lessons-our-emotions-can-teach-us-and-how-we-can-learn#1